Absolute Essentials of Environmental Economics

This shortform textbook provides a concise overview of the fundamentals of environmental economics. It focuses on how economic forces affect the natural environment and how economic policies and behaviors may be altered to improve environmental quality.

Spanning ten chapters, the book introduces readers to the key ideas in environmental economics. Topics include environmental externalities, technological change, cost-benefit analysis, pollution charges, emissions and offset trading, climate change, and public policy.

Written by an established educator and scholar, *Absolute Essentials of Environmental Economics* will be valuable reading for students of environmental economics, environmental policy, environmental management, and related areas. People affiliated with environmental interest groups, "think tanks," and advocacy groups will also find it beneficial.

Barry C. Field is Professor Emeritus of Resource Economics at the University of Massachusetts Amherst, USA.

With special thanks to Martha K. Field.

Absolute Essentials of Business and Economics

Textbooks are an extraordinarily useful tool for students and teachers, as is demonstrated by their continued use in the classroom and online. Successful textbooks run into multiple editions, and in endeavoring to keep up with developments in the field, it can be difficult to avoid increasing length and complexity.

This series of shortform textbooks offers a range of books which zero-in on the absolute essentials. In focusing on only the core elements of each sub-discipline, the books provide a useful alternative or supplement to traditional textbooks.

Absolute Essentials of Project Management
Paul Roberts

Absolute Essentials of Business Behavioural Ethics
Nina Seppala

Absolute Essentials of Corporate Governance
Stephen Bloomfield

Absolute Essentials of Business Ethics
Peter A. Stanwick & Sarah D. Stanwick

Absolute Essentials of Creative Thinking and Problem Solving
Tony Proctor

Absolute Essentials of Environmental Economics
Barry C. Field

For more information about this series, please visit: www.routledge.com/ Absolute-Essentials-of-Business-and-Economics/book-series/ABSOLUTE

Absolute Essentials of Environmental Economics

Barry C. Field

Routledge
Taylor & Francis Group

LONDON AND NEW YORK

First published 2022
by Routledge
2 Park Square, Milton Park, Abingdon, Oxon OX14 4RN

and by Routledge
605 Third Avenue, New York, NY 10158

Routledge is an imprint of the Taylor & Francis Group, an informa business

British Library Cataloguing-in-Publication Data
A catalogue record for this book is available from the British Library

Library of Congress Cataloging-in-Publication Data
A catalog record has been requested for this book

ISBN: 978-0-367-69794-5 (hbk)
ISBN: 978-1-032-12248-9 (pbk)
ISBN: 978-1-003-14363-5 (ebk)

DOI: 10.4324/9781003143635

Typeset in Times New Roman
by Deanta Global Publishing Services, Chennai, India

Contents

Contents

1 Introduction

ESSENTIAL SUMMARY

An economy is a set of institutions, relationships, and procedures by which a group of people seek to satisfy their needs and desires. The natural environment consists of the vast array of nonhuman processes and features that sustain and constrain human activity. Economists study the interaction of these two systems: how the environment affects the economy; how the economy affects the natural world. In this chapter we set out some basic concepts and understandings of this relationship as they have been addressed by economists and lay out the plan for the rest of the book.

Nature and the economy

Nature and the natural world have been providing sustenance, to humans, and constraints on human behavior, from the beginning. Also, from the beginning, humans have had impacts on the natural world. The interconnections were direct and obvious in early hunter/gatherer societies. They became even more obvious with the invention of agriculture. But now, with the massive growth of the urban industrial economy, they have become at the same time more extensive and, sometimes, more obscure.

Interaction between nature and humanity has played out both on the physical level, and at the level of thought. Nature has been an object of veneration and fear, a teacher of life lessons, a source of superstitions and hallucinations, and a supplier of philosophical premises.

Our mission in this book is to understand the physical interconnections between nature and the economy, and how this interconnection can be managed.

DOI: 10.4324/9781003143635-1

We can depict the essential physical linkages between the natural world and the world of humans with a simple diagram, shown in Figure 1.1. It displays the economy, consisting quite simply of collections of producers and consumers, as enclosed within an all-encompassing world of nature. There are two points of contact, a flow of "inputs" on the left, and a flow of leftovers, or "emissions" on the right. We discuss each in turn.

It is easy to understand the physical flows of inputs, the timber, ores, water, metals, etc., that flow in as virgin materials. Nature as a supplier of material inputs has had a prominent role in economics. Classical economists saw natural resource issues in the context of sustainability, the maintenance of economic growth and welfare in the face of growing scarcity of apparently critical natural resources. These concerns have been expressed continuously through the years, especially given the rapid demographic and economic growth of the twentieth century. For many years the analysis of natural resource supplies focused on accounting inventories and the resource sufficiency question: were there enough energy, timber, ores, water, etc., to supply an expanding industrial economy? Distinctions were made especially between renewable and non-renewable resources. Questions about the quantity of these inputs have historically been studied under the heading of natural resource economics. How should a given quantity of surface water be divided among users? How quickly should a given quantity, or perhaps an unknown quantity, of a depletable material be used? How fast should a timber harvest proceed in areas where it is possible to replant with new trees?

At the same time, our understanding of natural resources has evolved from lists of things that people use, and therefore apparently need, to natural

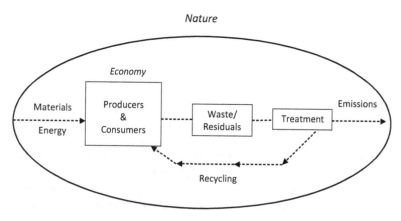

Figure 1.1 Economy and environment

resources as shifting elements of the natural world, the supplies and status of which are fundamentally shaped by the greatest resource of all: human ingenuity and creativity. Erich Zimmerman, in his famous 1933 work, wrote: "resources are not, they become; they are not static, but expand and contract in response to human wants and human actions." More recently the perspectives have been further broadened. One way was with the recognition of the non-consumptive use of resources. In many countries outdoor recreation has become an important growth industry. So the arrow on the left side of Figure 1.1 should be understood as referring also to non-consumptive resource use.

Another development has been a concern about natural resources and economic growth. Many countries possess what might be regarded as abundant supplies of natural resources of one type or another, yet are actually poor, and many have experienced low, or sometimes even negative growth rates. This has led to work on the question of whether, and how, the availability of natural resources has affected growth rates among the countries of the world. In a sense it reverses the classical concern: instead of thinking about the impact of growth on resource supplies, the concern here is the impact of resource availabilities on growth. One result of this is that the research boundaries normally encountered in the economic analysis have been substantially expanded. The work on "sustainability" has largely been done within the confines of standard neoclassical growth theory and application. The work on resources and growth, on the other hand, has reached out to bring in institutional, political, and social factors that often do not appear in the work of economists. As a reflection of this, there is now a broadened concern, among economists and others, to reconsider the whole notion of "natural capital."

Traditional models of resource use have been too much focused on maximizing measures of current GDP and have given insufficient attention to long-run changes in the stock of natural capital. Furthermore, natural capital needed to be defined more broadly, to include traditional resource uses, together with values that had historically been overlooked. The "stock" of natural capital must be seen to include resources in the classical sense, and the qualitative dimension of the natural environment, as impacted by the waste materials of the economy. A major preoccupation of ecological economics is the productivity of the natural world and the extent to which that productivity is degraded by the two links between nature and economy: the "raw materials" link and the "emissions" link. A way of thinking about this is by using a concept such as "ecological footprint" to represent the human impact on nature as a whole.

Part of that impact is the burden put on nature by the leftovers of the economy, especially the industrial economy of today. This directs our attention to the arrow on the right side of the diagram, marked "emissions." This represents the flow of waste materials and energy back into the natural environment. It is called environmental pollution, and it is the prime concern of what is called "environmental economics."

Pollution is not a new problem. Years ago, a local factory in my hometown was making paper and putting out smoke and wastewater that people in the town found noxious and unhealthy. They called meetings. They heard the plant owner explain how the smoke was a necessary result of their operation, and how costly it would be to cut it back, and how little it should be affecting people. They heard from some town's people about how unpleasant the smoke was. A local committee was formed and directed to study the problem. After everybody had had a say, the town government decided to try to walk the line between the effects of the pollution and the effects on the local economy. They got the plant owners to build a taller smokestack. Local issues like this still exist.

Environmental pollution control has become a more widespread problem. Human populations have grown into the billions. Material standards for many have vastly increased. Urbanization is strong throughout the world. Now environmental issues are addressed at all levels: local, regional, national, and global.

In Figure 1.1 we have shown a flow of waste materials/energy from the economy. From producers, the production of goods and services for consumers, and for other firms, yield waste streams. From consumers, waste includes energy flows, trash, and out-of-fashion consumer goods.

Waste flows into a box labeled "treatment." This stands for steps that can be taken to treat and transform the residuals from producers and consumers, into emissions that ultimately are returned to the environment. Treatment needs to be understood broadly. It may refer to the classic type of residuals like domestic sewage that is treated and rendered more benign. It may also refer to simply changing the time and season, or the location, of release to reduce the damage. The box labeled "treatment" refers to an "end-of-the-pipe" operation, since it lies between the initial waste flow and the environment.

The fundamental balance

According to the first law of thermodynamics, the energy and materials entering the economy cannot be made to disappear. They eventually must end up in the waste stream. The inputs of materials and energy on the left must equal, in the long run, the flow of residuals on the right side of the diagram. So in the long run, to reduce the flow of leftovers into the environment, it is necessary to reduce the inputs of energy and materials into the economy. It is to be emphasized that this is the long run. In the short run, some of the materials/energy will go toward expanding the size of the economic system. Materials will go into housing and infrastructure. Food will go into expanding the size of the population. So the most direct way of reducing the flow of residuals entering the environment is to have a smaller population. Of course, for most studies, the size of the population is taken as a given. But in individual countries, with changeable fertility rates and immigration/emigration flows, population growth may be an important variable. In fact, there is a well-regarded group within economics that studies the implications of zero population growth rates.

A second factor affecting the throughput of energy and materials is income, especially per capita income. Lower income levels mean lower levels of production and consumption. We have seen this vividly in the worldwide virus infection of 2020. The drop in per capita incomes led at that time to reductions in production and consumption, which led to substantial drops in pollution levels. Of course, in the modern world, progress is usually associated with higher income levels achieved through economic growth. This is especially the case among countries of the developing world.

It is possible to reduce the flow of waste from producers and consumers. This implies changing the system of production and consumption to reduce the overall amounts of waste produced per unit of total output. The term for this is "pollution prevention," and it comes about through lowering the "waste intensity" of production/consumption, that is, the amount of waste generated per unit of output. In most developed countries there has been a pronounced shift in production and consumption, from material goods to services. The production of material goods normally involves greater physical waste per unit than the production of services. Thus, the shift from goods to services has produced over time a decrease in the waste intensity of the economy as a whole, thereby leading to lower levels of waste production.

We then come to recycling, an activity that is almost automatic in countries of the developed world, and which has grown in popularity and perspective within the developing world. Recycling means reaching into the waste stream to extract materials and energy that may be redirected back into production/consumption.

Finally, we come to waste treatment and management. How waste is managed has important implications for the damage it causes. Waste treatment processes can substantially change the toxicity of waste materials. Waste flows can be altered in time and place, thereby changing the damage they cause. A vital part of the economics of pollution control centers on the conditions that affect the development over time of new pollution-control technologies.

Environmental economics

The discussion above related to the objectives and principles of what has been called the "circular economy." This is sometimes looked at as an engineering problem of laying out certain paths and technologies of materials handling. But it is actually an economic problem, or rather a sequence of economic problems, by which we mean a sequence of places where there is a trade-off between means and technologies, which can only be resolved by reference to the values humans place on alternatives and outcomes and by the incentives they face in those situations. To move to different places in these trade-offs, two things are required: changes in attitudes and understandings about human behavior and their environmental impacts, and changes in the incentives people face in the decisions they make that have environmental impacts. Environmental economics is the study of these relationships.

Environmental economics as a systematic and specialized topic for studying these matters began in the mid-twentieth century. Since then, it has developed into a voluminous and sophisticated body of work covering all dimensions of the interaction between the economy and the environment and at all levels, local, regional, national, and global. This book presents the rudiments of that topic. It covers the basic concepts and principles of the discipline. It is short, so it cannot cover everything. Rather it focuses on the basic ideas.

There are two dimensions of economics, and therefore two dimensions of environmental economics: what is, and what should be. The first of these is an analytical focus or how things are related, how causal linkages connect different parts of the economy and the environment. If 50 percent of the cars on the road were switched to electric vehicles, how much would air pollution decrease? If people were charged for the carbon content of their purchases, how much would consumption diminish? The second task is about policy and involves the word "should." What should we strive for in terms of cleaner water? What should people and countries do to slow up global climate change?

Economists bring to the study of the environment the standard analytical tools of the trade. These are based on two leading ideas:

- The first is that in a situation of scarcity relative to human wants we are required to make decisions involving trade-offs, when more of one thing means having less of something else.
- The second is that the terms of the trade-off can be altered, by changes in the wants and needs of people themselves, and by new technological developments that give us new ways of managing the flows of materials and energy.

Environmental economics also emphasizes the legal and economic incentives that shape peoples' behavior. An incentive is a reward or a penalty that inheres in a decision situation and leads people to prefer one course of action over another. A legal incentive is simply based on the notion of something that is encouraged, or discouraged, through regulations that have potential penalties when violated. An economic incentive is the way a decision situation is structured to create a reward, positive or negative, for the person making the decision.

In this, the profession relies heavily on theories of how individuals might behave in certain situations, not strictly on a description of these actions. Some people may be impatient with this. It may seem to be wrapped up in ideas that appear not to have a lot of day-to-day significance. But what paying attention to principles and theory does is to allow a person to cut through the noise and dust of policy conflict to see and comprehend the basic structure of the problems under consideration.

There are a number of variants and extensions of economics and environmental economics, for example behavioral economics, ecological economics, sustainability economics, and experimental economics. We will refer to these when necessary, but the primary thrust of the book is the main corpus of concepts and relationships comprising mainstream environmental economics.

Environmental economics and morality

Environmental economics is based on a study of the incentives, economic and otherwise, that lead people to act as they do. Yet the environment has also a moral and ethical foundation. Many people feel that nature and natural features are in some sense gifts to humans, who feel a moral imperative for preserving and encouraging them in a world where economic security has become a prime motive and economic growth a fixation. However, nature and humanity are inextricably intertwined; no part of the "natural" world has escaped human impact. So a moral judgment on nature is, ipso facto, a judgment on humanity. These thoughts lie behind the modern concept of an environmental bill of rights, that humans have a right to live in a healthy natural environment. But a statement of rights doesn't automatically confer on someone the power to obtain and hold the thing in question, nor does it tell us what to do if several types of rights conflict.

A rights or power issue is behind the modern notion that aspects of features of the natural environment have a legal right to existence and protection. This notion has actually seeped into areas of environmental (and natural resource) policy. In the United States, the Endangered Species Act commits the government to protect species irrespective of their direct utility to humans. And the Comprehensive Environmental Response, Compensation, and Liability Act requires that certain damaged resources be restored to their original condition, again irrespective of their direct utility to humans. Some communities around the world have adopted local laws that recognize legal rights for certain natural resource features.

There is another important connection between environmental pollution control and environmental ethics. This is the question of the circumstances in which society might call on, or rely on, moral attitudes as an instrumental means to control pollution. As mentioned above, conventional environmental economics is about legal or market incentives that will bring polluters to reduce their emissions. But there may be some circumstances where it may be more effective to allow, or encourage, people to express, and act upon, their moral attitudes against pollution. One situation is when standard monitoring and enforcement are too costly, for example litter that is causally dropped over an area too large effectively to monitor. Another is when people enter into a collective agreement for which there is no means of monitoring performance. Another is a situation in which performance can be monitored but there is no way for some authority to enforce performance. This fits the problem of adopting international agreements for global pollution reduction.

Regulatory enforcement is a costly function, and there will always be questions of resource use; whether more resources devoted to enforcement will produce enough additional compliance to be worth it. One would expect these resources to be more productive the more pervasive the ethical attitude in society in favor of a cleaner natural environment. Most of us would prefer to live in a world where there is an ample supply of moral capital even if we feel we must rely for the most part on incentives of one type or another. But an unfortunate part of morality is that it may not be as widespread as we would like, and there is no assured way of producing more of it.

Plan for the book

The book begins with a discussion of how environmental impacts originate, especially in market economics. This is the principle of environmental externalities. It then turns, in Chapter 3, to a very general model of the way short-run environmental protection decisions present themselves: as a trade-off of environmental damages and the social costs of rectifying them. Chapter 4 is a discussion of factors underlying long-run decisions, primarily the factors affecting changes in pollution-control technologies over time. Chapter 5 is a discussion of ideas that economists use to assess the damages that environmental pollution causes. Chapter 6 is a very short review of some of the issues and institutions that affect the policy world, that is, the world where public decisions are made regarding steps to protect the natural environment. Chapters 7, 8, and 9 each deal with a certain type of environmental pollution control procedure, namely, standards, emissions taxes or charges, and emissions trading. Chapter 10 deals with the basic economics of what has become the primary contemporary pollution-control issue: global climate change.

Terminology

Environmental economics, like any specialized form of inquiry, has its own terminology. We will use the following terms throughout the book:

Residuals: materials and energy that are left over after production or consumption
Emissions: materials and energy that are introduced into the environment
Damages: the negative impacts on society stemming from emissions
Pollutant: the material or energy that cause damages when introduced into the environment
Ambient quality: the concentration of a pollutant in the environment (e.g., parts per million of SO_2 in the air, or chemical in the water)
Recycling: the process of returning production or consumption materials back into the system to be used again for production and/or consumption

How to use this book

This book discusses the rudiments of environmental economics. It covers the leading ideas of the subject, but it is not intended as a stand-alone text. It should be useful as a supplement to courses on environmental economics, to give students an overall view of the topic before they are led into the details of each concept and principle. The book should also be useful to those who struggle in the environmental policy arena, and who wish to know more about the topic without having to go so far as to enroll in a course or read a standard text. The book should be helpful for gaining a general understanding of current issues in environmental management, too. And it fits as a primer for people following developments in popular environmental topics.

References and further reading

Hawken, P., et al. (2005), *Natural Capitalism: The Next Industrial Revolution*, Routledge, London.
Huber, C., et al. (2019), *Sustaining Environmental Capital Initiative Summary Report*, U.S. Geological Survey Open File Report Number 2019-1117, Geological Survey, Washington, DC.

Krutilla, J. (1967), "Conservation Reconsidered," *American Economic Review*, Volume 57, Number 4, pp. 777–786.

Segerson, K. (2010), *The Economics of Pollution Control*, Edward Elgar, Cheltenham, UK and Northampton, MA.

Zimmerman, E.W. (1933), *World Resources and Industries*, Harper, London.

2 Markets and environmental pollution

ESSENTIAL SUMMARY

This book is about the economics of pollution control. Economics is conventionally divided into microeconomics and macroeconomics. The bulk of what we will cover is micro in perspective: how polluting firms can be regulated effectively to reduce their environmental impacts. Some of our concerns will be with collections of firms, for example all coal-fired power plants or all-new fossil-fueled cars. In a later chapter on climate change, our prime subjects will be the nation states of the world. Most countries rely on markets to govern the production and distribution of goods and services to consumers. Private markets, in which buyers and sellers negotiate terms of transactions, very often produce environmental externalities. An externality is an effect flowing from a market but is not taken into account by the participants in that market. In this chapter, we discuss the concept of environmental externalities and the types of externalities that occur. This is in preparation for later chapters dealing with the ways markets may be regulated to reduce or eliminate environmental pollution.

Markets and environmental externalities

Most countries of the world use markets to direct the flow of goods and services among producers and consumers. A market is a social institution in which individuals or groups come together to negotiate and transact the ownership and use of goods and services. All markets function within a set of rules, customs, and standard procedures. In many countries of the west, markets are allowed to operate relatively independently of political forces. In other countries, markets are subject to various political controls.

DOI: 10.4324/9781003143635-2

In all countries, markets are subject to moral and ethical motivations and influences.

The standard way of understanding a market is by examining the behavior of the two main participants: demanders and suppliers. In a classical market, suppliers are the producers who manufacture a good, or people who control access to some service. Often suppliers come to the market with preconceived ideas about an acceptable price for their product. Demanders are those who come to procure the good or service at prices that are acceptable to them. We depict the prospects facing suppliers and demanders with supply curves and demand curves. Consider the relationships pictured in Figure 2.1. For the moment look only at the solid lines, one labeled S and the other D. These are the familiar supply and demand curves of microeconomics. The demand curve shows the quantities of the good or service that consumers would wish to obtain at alternative prices. The downward slope of D indicates that this quantity will be greater the lower the price is at which it can be obtained. The demand curve is a pictorial representation of the value that consumers place on the good or service in question. The supply curve is the quantity of the item that would be made available by suppliers at alternative prices. It's upward sloping: the higher the price the greater the quantity that would be made available by suppliers. The supply curve is a pictorial representation of costs that suppliers would encounter in producing and making available the good or service. If we now suppose a situation in which buyers and sellers can interact without hinderance, we could

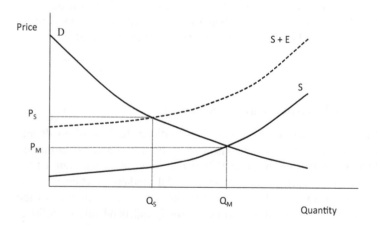

Figure 2.1 Typical market supply and demand

expect that the natural forces of competition would lead in this market to the price and quantity that simultaneously satisfy buyers and sellers.

Looking at the demand and supply curves of Figure 2.1 may lead one to think of markets as static entities where prices and quantities settled down to "equilibrium" levels. But the real world is dynamic, subject to constant change. On the supply side, production technologies change, which pictorially would shift the supply relationship outward, an increase. We will see that in environmental pollution control, technologies are in constant change, as we find new ways of producing with fewer leftovers or waste, or new ways of handling waste.

The factors that affect demand are also subject to constant change: populations expand in numbers, and sometimes decline. Incomes grow or shrink. Tastes and preferences shift over time. As incomes increase, and people's basic needs are met, they ordinarily have a greater preference for pollution-free lifestyles. So in the real world we may never actually see prices and quantities settle down to some long-run static equilibrium. Nevertheless, the simple supply and demand relationships give us a way of thinking about the economic forces that are at work and the directions in which they are pushing events.

We need some way of evaluating the social performance of markets, of deciding whether they are performing well or badly in specific instances. The major criterion is efficiency. A market is performing efficiently if it brings into balance the forces of supply and demand. The efficient price in the price graph is given by the intersection of the demand and supply curves. It does not mean that demanders would not like a lower price and suppliers a higher one. It means only that there is a balance between the two sides of the market. At the efficient price, the quantity demanded by buyers is the same as the quantity supplied by producers; there is no shortage or surplus. We will use the concept of efficiency to evaluate environmental regulations that have the objective of reducing environmental pollution.

To achieve efficiency there must be competition among suppliers and among demanders. Markets can be inefficient because of monopoly (one supplier) or an oligopoly (several suppliers who collude among themselves). Markets can be inefficient because of a monopsony (one demander, for example in a "company town"), or oligopsony (several colluding demanders). Efficiency requires that both demanders and suppliers have full information about the good or service at issue. If suppliers have better knowledge about the good or service (e.g., in used cars), or if demanders have better information than suppliers (e.g., in home insurance), then markets will be inefficient.

Another important criterion for evaluating a market is economic equity or fairness. An efficient price may or may not be regarded as fair, or equitable. A judgment on the fairness of a market requires a wider look at the conditions outside the market itself. We will discuss this at greater length when we come to environmental equity, often referred to as environmental justice. Environmental justice is the notion that disadvantaged members of society, such as those with low and moderate incomes, should not be disproportionately exposed to environmental pollution. It stemmed from the observation that polluted sites, such as chemical disposal sites, are often located near low-income neighborhoods. It also includes the idea that low-income people ought not to be disproportionately burdened with the costs of pollution reduction.

Another issue in which fairness must be addressed is using pollution taxes to control carbon emissions. In recent years, economists, and others, have recommended placing a price on carbon to motivate people to lower their carbon footprint. Objections have been raised that the higher prices for goods and services this would cause would be unjust for low-income consumers. However, there are ways to avoid this. We will discuss this topic in later chapters.

Another equity question is whether a dollar (or pound, or euro, or any other currency) of environmental quality is to be treated as equal in value to a dollar of conventional economic output. This could simply be a matter of the scale used to evaluate a unit of environmental quality. Or it could be an objection to putting any monetary value on elements of the natural environment – the idea that they have a value that can never truly be captured by a price.

External costs

Supply curves originate in production costs. The upward slope shows the ordinary case, where production costs rise with the rate of output. These would be private costs, in the sense that they are the costs that show up on the profit and loss statements of the supplying firms. Suppose there are some other costs involved in producing an item, and, in fact, that these are certain environmental costs, perhaps downstream water pollution or downwind air pollution resulting from the actions of the producer. These are true costs to somebody in society, but they don't appear in the income statements of the firm. They are what we call external costs; costs that are real but are external to the entities (private firms, non-profit firms, government agencies, etc.) that are making the production decisions.

The concept of external costs is fundamental in the study of environmental economics because environmental costs are almost always external costs. Controlling the environmental damage of a system means controlling the external costs stemming from production within that system. Refer to Figure 2.1. Suppose the producing entities in this system are responsible for certain downwind air pollution costs (ill-health of people living downwind, for example). If we want to account for the total costs to all of society of producing this item, we must add the external environmental costs to the private costs shown by the standard supply curve. This is shown by the dotted line in the diagram labeled S+E. It lies above the original supply curve by an amount equal to the external environmental costs (E).

Most, but not necessarily all, environmental externalities involve some physical linkage between those responsible for the externality and those affected by it. For example, the diminished water quality in a lake, air that has a high content of particulate matter, an airport where departing aircraft produce noise, and so on. Environmental externalities are sometimes obvious, and sometimes not. A polluted lake or river may be easy to see and smell. Polluted air may diminish scenic views and discomfort lungs. But some externalities may be unknown, such as the CO_2 context of the surrounding atmosphere. Sometimes people become habituated to externalities, such as certain noise pollution. There are externalities that do not involve direct linkage, such as when buildings or roads are located on scenic vistas.

Full social efficiency in a market requires equality between demand and all costs, including both private and external (environmental) costs. Recall that total social costs are the private costs plus the external costs. The socially efficient output level is shown by Q_s in Figure 2.1, while the privately efficient market output, that is the output that maximizes the net incomes of the private firms in the market, is Q_M. Hence in an unregulated market in which environmental externalities exist, the output of the good or service will be too high ($Q_M > Q_s$), and the price too low ($P_M < P_s$), relative to the socially efficient levels. We have discussed these externalities as effects stemming from markets. This may give the impression that private markets are the only place where environmental impacts occur. However, public organizations can also produce externalities. An environmental externality is an impact that is disregarded by authorities in charge of the entity. For example, public utilities, set up to provide water and power, are often a source of environmental externalities. And military establishments have often had substantial impacts on air, water, and soil.

We can now understand that environmental policy is primarily a matter of dealing with these externalities. There is in Figure 2.1 another feature of importance. The externality in that case is roughly proportional to the quantity of output. Here, the only way of getting rid of the externality completely may be to end the production of the item involved. This sometimes happens in the real world but often does not. Instead there are ways of reducing externalities without having to stop production. This leads us to the conclusion that reducing environmental externalities is not a free good; there is a cost involved. It is a cost that many people will willingly bear, but it is a cost, nevertheless.

Varieties of environmental externalities

Environmental externalities are the impacts on the environment that are disregarded by the people who are causing them. There are many different types of them, based especially on their physical characteristics. And these features have a great bearing on how they can be addressed and resolved in the world of environmental policy.

Local vs. regional vs. global

Local impacts are confined to a small area, usually in the vicinity of the people who caused them. Examples are local air pollution caused by small manufacturing enterprises, the local impact of woodstoves, or the contamination of a nearby water body from domestic waste. Regional impacts occur over larger distances, through wind patterns, rivers, and the like. Particularly relevant are regional impacts that cross national borders. Climate change has confronted us now with an externality that is truly global in extent. The locational extent of an environmental externality is obviously critical in being able to manage it because collective action at the local level is likely to be more effective than national or international action. An important factor at the local level is whether the externality is from a single source or from multiple sources.

Uniformly vs. non-uniformly mixed emissions

Industrial pollutants are often uniformly mixed; the emissions from one source mix together with, and become indistinguishable from, emissions from other sources. When emissions mix together like this it is very difficult to distinguish the damage caused by one source from that caused by other sources. Pollution abatement regulations have to be structured accordingly. When the contribution of different sources can be identified, especially when it is something like the contamination of local water resources, regulation can be tailored to match.

Cumulative vs. non-cumulative

Many externalities are cumulative, in the sense that current emissions continue to add to the stock of pollutants from previous days or years. Some are non-cumulative and dissipate immediately, like noise pollution, for example. Another way to think about this is that some pollutants are persistent; they do not immediately dissipate. The rate of persistence may vary. Certain biological emissions into water may degrade fairly quickly depending on the oxygen level of the water. Similarly, different substances emitted into the atmosphere will degrade relatively quickly, while others will not, so the rate of accumulation is different for each one.

Continuous vs. episodic

Many industrial emissions are continuous; they happen as long as the source is in operation. Some are episodic and occur sporadically, for example, accidental spills or unscheduled temporary releases, such as unexpected flooding. At issue here is the availability and management of emergency response resources. The degree of risk is inherent in the phenomenon under consideration, and an important issue is how people value the benefits of reducing the risk. This blends into virtually all environmental externalities that extend over time because we are usually not sure about the degree of risk we face from future events.

Point source vs. non-point source

The location where a pollutant actually enters the environment is important. Some, called non-point source, such as the run-off of agricultural chemicals, are diffuse and therefore hard to measure. Also it may be difficult to identify their exact originating point. Point-source pollutants, that stem from a recognizable outfall, such as a chimney or water pipes, are easier to monitor and control.

Toxic vs. non-toxic

Toxic and non-toxic releases have to do with the physical and chemical nature of the emission. This is not the same as emissions being damaging or not. Excessive amounts of non-toxic material can be damaging. For some chemicals, the "damage is in the dose," i.e., small doses may be reasonably benign, while large doses are toxic. This is a frequent problem with chemicals. Modern economies use thousands of different chemicals for thousands of different uses. Some of these are used without a thorough knowledge of their possible toxicity. So we are faced with managing externalities of unknown extent.

Public goods

If people in general put a high value on having a non-polluted natural environment, why do we not see private firms cleaning up portions of the environment, and then selling their service to the people who have benefited? For example, consider people who live along the banks of a river. If there was a possibility of making a profit from this, why wouldn't a private firm clean up the river? Suppose we know that each person along the river would be willing to pay 100 euros to have the river water cleaned up. And suppose there are 100 such homeowners. Suppose the firm cleans up the river (at a cost of 5,000 euros) and then sends an invoice of 100 euros to each homeowner. How many of these homeowners would pay the invoice? Some would pay, no doubt. But many would not. It's different from buying food at a shop. In that case, if they don't pay, they don't get the food. But in the case of the river cleanup, they might be motivated to withhold payment, or pay a small amount, and still enjoy the cleaned-up river. The point is that cleaning up the river is what, in economics, is called a public good. A public good in this case is a good, or service, which when made available to one person is automatically available to others. The cleaning of the river cannot be done for one homeowner without being made available to all others living on the river. The homeowners understand this, of course, and many of them will react as "free riders," enjoying the benefits but not paying their share of the costs. With an incentive to free ride among the homeowners, there is no incentive for private firms to provide the service.

Cleaning up the environment is a public good. We cannot expect private markets to produce efficient quantities of this "good." All the more reason why an economy composed of private firms will normally underprovide, or provide too little, environmental quality control. All the more reason why, if these externalities are to get remedied, we must resort to some form of public regulation to accomplish it.

Public goods produce an incentive to free ride. A free rider is one who stands to reap the benefits of a public good without sacrificing their share of its costs. The quality of the earth's atmosphere, in terms of the CO_2 content, is a public good, in this case a global public good. If a single country were to take steps to reduce its CO_2 emissions, all countries would benefit, not just the one that reduced the emissions. The upshot of this is that in addressing global pollution, there exists an incentive for countries to free ride. This is not to say that nothing will ever be done. Only that in taking steps to achieve global atmospheric pollution reduction, countries will have to deal with the free-riding incentive.

If public goods, like a less polluted or cleaner environment, are to be provided at a socially efficient level, some type of collective action is necessary. Collective action means connected or coordinated action by members of a group. Usually this is done through a government organization or agency; however, in some cases, it could be a privately organized group. With public goods, free riding is not the only issue that requires a collective response. The amount of clean-up will be the same for everybody. But people may differ in terms of what level of public good they think would be best. Some people on the river want a river with pristine water quality, some others would be happy with less. Collective action will be required to rectify these differences.

Open-access externalities

With certain types of depletable natural resources, there are externalities that individual users inflict upon each other when they have uncontrolled access to a relatively limited quantity of a natural resource. The classic example is grazing sheep on a pasture of limited acreage. Each shepherd, in evaluating the size of the flock they will graze on the pasture, would, at the margin, evaluate the benefits and costs to themselves of adding (or subtracting) one more animal to the pasture. They ordinarily would not consider the cost they would be inflicting on other shepherds in the form of decreasing the availability of grass for animals already on the pasture. These are called open-access externalities and lead to overuse of the resource. A similar phenomenon exists in open-access fisheries. (And in the choice of wearing a mask in an epidemic: the depletable resource in this case is a virus-free atmosphere. In deciding whether or not to don a mask, a perfectly selfish individual would not take into account the fact that, if they refused to put on a face mask, they would be reducing the supply of this depletable resource for others in their vicinity.)

The macro look

The bulk of what we will cover in this book is the microeconomics of pollution control. It deals with the regulation of polluting entities, mostly private firms. Macroeconomics deals with the behavior of national economies as a single unit. The most familiar macroeconomic concept is Gross Domestic Product (GDP) which is a measure of the total output of final goods and services produced within the borders of a country during a particular time, usually a year.

The growth rate of GDP is a particularly important factor because, together with the growth rate of population, it determines the extent to which standards of living may change. And this is important because of the well-known relationship of GDP growth and citizen demands for a cleaner environment. This is normally a positive relationship: higher standards of living, as in higher GDP per capita, usually lead to greater demands for improved environmental quality.

Shifts in the sectoral makeup of economies also have had important implications for their macro environmental impacts. Developed economies, such as those of western Europe and North America, have service sectors that are growing faster than traditional manufacturing sectors. This means a shift away from more heavily polluting industries and an expansion of sectors with smaller pollution footprints.

Still another case where a macroeconomic perspective is important is in predicting the overall future economic impact of global climate change. There is wide agreement that this impact will be large. But how best to express it? Most efforts express the cost of climate change in terms of the amount by which expected future GDP will be lower as a result of climate change. The damages from climate change, in other words, are measured in terms of lost future income.

A macroeconomic concept of great concern is the distribution of income, especially whether it is changing over time, toward greater, or lesser, equality. Mirroring that is the issue of whether environmental pollution is distributed more or less equally. It is a matter of equity whether citizens with higher incomes are exposed to lower levels of pollution, or to say it the opposite way, whether low-income citizens tend, on average, to live and work in more heavily polluted environments. Distributional issues can, of course, be addressed at the international level. A major issue in reaching international agreements on environmental matters is how they may differentially affect rich and poor countries.

We have concluded that private markets will often lead to environmental pollution. This has suggested to some that to get rid of pollution we must get rid of markets. But private markets are an important institution. In modern economies, they offer producers and consumers a way of solving the complex problems of production and distribution of millions of goods and services. It is not markets that lead to pollution, but unregulated markets. It will happen wherever there are environmental effects that are ignored by the people who cause them. Our focus in these coming pages will be on how public regulation can be fashioned so as to bring about the efficient management of environmental externalities.

Further reading

Banzhaf, S., et al. (2019), "Environmental Justice: The Economies of Race, Place, and Pollution," *Journal of Economic Perspectives*, Volume 33, Number 1, pp. 185–208.

Coarse, R.H. (1960), "The Problem of Social Cost," *Journal of Law and Economics*, Volume 3, pp. 1–44.

Field, B.C. and M.K. Field (2021), *Environmental Economics An Introduction*, The McGraw-Hill Companies, New York.

Helm, D. ed. (1991), *Economic Policy Towards the Environment*, Blackwell Publishing, London.

3 The basic economics of environmental pollution control

ESSENTIAL SUMMARY

In this chapter, we discuss the basic model of pollution control economics, the trade-off between pollution damages to society and the social costs of pollution control. We explain the concepts of the marginal damages of pollution and the marginal abatement costs of reducing pollution. With these we develop the concept of the socially efficient level of pollution control. This sets the stage for a later discussion of the policy alternatives for attaining this efficiency point. We also address the issue of whether the efficient level of pollution control is also the most equitable. In Chapter 2, we explained why unregulated private markets will produce too much environmental pollution. For some people this might mean any amount greater than zero. Others might have a different point of view. Here, we will use the notion of social efficiency: the level of pollution control that balances, on the margin, the damages stemming from pollution with the costs of controlling this pollution.

Pollution damages

We are going to conceptualize the pollution control issues facing any group of people as a trade-off, or balance, between the damages caused by pollution and the social costs of reducing that pollution. We have a defined group of people, and a defined quantity of pollution. Remember that pollution can be associated with a given amount of emissions, or a given amount of ambient pollutant.

By damages we mean all the negative effects of a particular pollutant, for example, the ill effects stemming from power plant SO_2 emissions, or the effects of noise generated by traffic on a nearby highway, or those from the

DOI: 10.4324/9781003143635-3

accumulation of carbon dioxide in the earth's atmosphere. Some of these damages are health related, such as the effects on human morbidity and mortality of exposure to pollutants in the atmosphere. Some may be damage to materials, e.g., corrosion and wear on buildings. Some may be agricultural damages, such as the negative effects of air pollutants on crop yields. Some may be damage to ecosystems, e.g., acidification of lakes and streams and the damage this implies to wildlife. For the moment, don't be concerned with how we could actually measure these damages. That's hugely important, and it will be covered in Chapter 5.

In Figure 3.1, damages are represented pictorially by the line labeled MD. MD stands for marginal damages. (For the moment, ignore the dashed line in the figure.) Marginal means the added damage costs produced by one more unit of pollution. The scale on the vertical axis is a scale of value. Typically this value is expressed in terms of a monetary unit. This does not mean that the only things that count are things that have market prices. We will see that many factors on the damage side are non-market values. Marginal damages are defined as the reduced damages stemming from one fewer unit of emissions. Note again that the horizontal axis measures emissions. We could also imagine a damage function related to ambient conditions. A move to the right would then depict more polluted ambient conditions, and MD would be marginal damages from a diminished ambient environment. There are many factors that lie behind damage functions. For example, as populations increase downwind or downstream, any level of emissions will produce greater damages. We will discuss these types of factors later in the chapter.

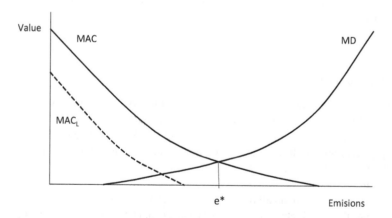

Figure 3.1 Efficient level of emissions

The marginal damage function includes all damages to society, that is, all damages of whatever sort and to whomever they are occurring. It is drawn as swinging upward to the right. Its height and specific shape will vary according to which particular pollutant we are discussing. As drawn, it increases slowly at low emission levels. Then as these levels increase it turns upward. For higher emission levels, damages are depicted as increasing rapidly. The one pictured, for example, displays what is called a "threshold," small levels of emissions that produce no damages. Some pollutants do not have thresholds: damages start, and may be very high, right from the beginning. Determining the damages from various pollutants under various circumstances is the work of health scientists, epidemiologists, and others. The role of economists is to find ways to render the physical damage estimates into terms whereby they may be added up and combined with one another, and with other social objectives. In the ongoing controversies over environmental regulations, major conflicts happen over what is, in effect, the shape of the damage function for particular pollutants in particular circumstances.

Of course, the nature of damages depends on the type of emissions and the effect they have on the ambient environment. If what are involved are strictly non-accumulating pollutants, the damages are confined to people currently alive. If these emissions were to cease, the damages would also stop. But if these are accumulating stock pollutants, current emissions add to the material already there, adding to the damage to current generations but also to damages to future generations. An example is chemicals contaminating an aquifer and dissipating, if at all, only over a very long time period. Global climate change from accumulated atmospheric carbon is another example.

Pollution abatement costs

On the other side of damages is the curve showing marginal abatement costs (MAC). Abatement costs are the costs of reducing emissions. This is also a marginal curve; it shows the marginal or added costs of reducing emissions by a unit, for example by one tonne of carbon dioxide or by one part per million for a chemical in water. MAC goes upward to the left. The logic is that under normal circumstances it's fairly inexpensive to reduce emissions when they are high; it's much more costly to cut emissions when they are already low. A marginal abatement cost relationship (and, of course, the associated marginal damage function) can apply to any type of emission situation, for example to a country that wishes to reduce its national CO_2 emissions, a region within a country, a group of firms comprising a defined industry, even to reducing the carbon footprint of an individual.

A marginal abatement cost function is meant to refer to the most cost-effective way of reducing emissions. Cost-effectiveness means getting the biggest impact for the amount spent. When multiple sources are involved, a collective decision is required. A typical source in a polluting industry may have numerous methods and technologies available for reducing emissions. Some of these might be end-of-pipe measures for dealing with residuals; others might involve substantial changes in production processes. Having each source reduce their emissions by the same amount, or in the same proportion, may not be the most cost-effective way to achieve pollution reduction. If some sources have lower costs than others a collective pollution-control program needs to take advantage of these differences to be fully cost-effective.

Suppose we are trying to control emissions from a group of two power plants. It needs to be worked out how a total reduction will be distributed among the two plants. Suppose currently, each plant emits 20 tonnes of pollutants. And we wish to reduce the total from 40 tonnes to 20 tonnes. For political reasons it might be decided to get each plant to reduce emissions to 10 tonnes. If the emission reduction costs vary, such as $10 per tonne in the first plant and $2 per tonne in the second, this equi-proportionate rule would imply total emission control costs of $240. But if you have the second plant (the one with lower abatement costs) cut back by 20 tonnes and the other plant by nothing, then the overall cost of reducing emissions would be $80, a big saving to society over the equi-proportionate method. These numbers are merely to identify an important principle: when there are sources with markedly different emission control costs, it is impossible to put together a fully cost-effective pollution-control program unless regulators take advantage of these differences.

We now have both actors on stage: MD and MAC. Considering the two sides of the situation we now can identify the socially optimal level of emissions. It is e*, the emissions level that equates MD and MAC. e* is the emission level that minimizes the cost of pollution. If emissions exceed this, marginal damages will exceed marginal abatement costs, and the overall social cost can be lowered by decreasing emissions. If emissions are below e*, abatement costs are too high relative to damages so total social costs can be decreased with an increase in emissions. What we have looks suspiciously like a supply and demand diagram. But there is a difference. The supply and demand curves in a market show how two groups of people will interact, making transactions that will tend to drive the market price to an equilibrium. In MD and MAC curves, we have two groups of people, those who suffer damages from pollution and those who can abate it. If a small number of people are involved on each side and they can sit down and negotiate, they may be able to decide on the optimal emission rate. But in a typical pollution control situation, involving large numbers of people, there is nothing to suggest that that these two groups will be able to get together and negotiate an effective solution to the pollution problem.

The concept may be hard to accept. Why aren't optimal emissions zero? For some types of pollutants they may be zero. If the graph referred to a highly toxic material, the damage function might be much higher than the one pictured. It might be so high that the curves don't intersect. Pictorially that means that e* would actually be located at the vertical axis. The optimal level of emissions would be zero because the cost of pushing emissions to zero is less than the reduction in damages.

Examples of the MD/MAC model

Example A: suppose there is a small lake, where a dozen families live around the shores. On the far end of the lake a small brewery operates. The brewery emits a small stream of liquid waste into the lake. It is easy to see the two sides in this case. The brewery faces some emission abatement costs from steps taken to reduce the outflow. The homeowners face damages from the diminished quality of the lake water. The damages could be health related: possible diseases stemming from exposure to contaminated water. Also, they could be partly aesthetic: smelly water.

Example B: consider a somewhat more complicated situation. A group of old, coal-fired power plants emit, from their tall stacks, particulate-ladened air pollutants that drift hundreds of miles downwind. The people living downwind suffer the health-related damages, such as asthma, caused by the emissions. The damage function in this case shows the value of the damages as they relate to the quantity of emissions from the plants. The abatement cost function shows how much it would cost to reduce emissions from the plants, with modest costs for small reductions and increasing as the reductions get bigger to reflect the technical options for reducing emissions.

Example C: consider an even more complicated situation: plastic. The US and other developed countries each produce hundreds of millions of plastic items, which get dispersed throughout the economy. Every year a huge quantity of plastic is collected after use through various channels to become waste. Much of it is shipped to other countries for disposal. A lot of it was sent to China, until 2017 when that route was shut off; shipments then shifted to other destinations, particularly African and Southeast Asian countries. There it is disposed of in ways that expose a lot of people to accumulating plastic disposal sites, legal and illegal. The damage function in this case shows the health, aesthetic, and ecosystem damages, stemming from accumulating plastic. On the other side, abatement costs relate to the cost in the US of collecting the plastic material and either recycling it or disposing of it in non-damaging ways, or the costs of switching to non-plastic substitutes. The interesting aspect of this case is that the people who suffer damages and the people who would incur the abatement costs are in different countries. Here e* becomes an international affair, with all the political complications this implies.

Does this approach privilege pollution control costs over the damages that pollution causes? It does not. Our interest in environmental economics, and policy, undoubtedly stems from the felt notion that current pollution levels are way above e*. The model contains the notion that in reducing emissions levels, society should be concerned both with what we gain by so doing, and what we must forego.

One could say that e* is a social aspiration level, considering all of the damages and abatement costs that this particular pollutant involves. However, e* is essentially a public good. Although the particular "public" that is involved will differ from case to case, e* will be the same for everybody in the group. Some individuals may desire an emission level lower than e*; some people, for example the polluters themselves, would likely regard e* as too low because of the costs of attaining it. In the real world of pollution-control politics, there will be a conflict over where e* should be. Much of it will hinge on where the MAC and MD curves are actually located. So, finding and interpreting data about MD and MAC is of supreme importance. We focus on this problem in Chapter 5.

Time

One real issue in establishing e* is with time. In many cases, global climate change, for example, the costs are near in time while the damages and damage reduction occur well into the future. Thus MAC and MD come with totally different time signatures. How do we compare a euro's worth of abatement costs today with a euro's worth of reduced damages 10 or 20 years in the future? This is the vexing problem of discounting, which we will discuss in Chapter 5.

Equity

According to our definitions, e* is the efficient level of emissions. But is e* also fair, or equitable? The group suffering damages is normally not the one that is responsible for the emissions, or for abating them. One type of equity question is, who is primarily responsible for pollution? We saw in Chapter 1 that the total flow of polluting residuals can be divided between that coming from firms and that coming from households. Some types of emissions come mainly from firms (e.g., SO_2 from powerplants) and some mainly from households (e.g., car tail-pipe emissions). Critiques differ about where to put primary responsibility: polluting firms or polluting households. At the international level, the problem is to come to some agreement on how the total pollution abatement effort should be distributed among countries.

Another equity issue is how the total reduction in emissions is divided among all the firms in the industry. It may seem fair that all firms are treated alike. So if regulators desire a cutback in total industry emissions of 50 percent, then the equitable thing to do would be to have each firm in that industry reduce their emissions by 50 percent. But this might not be regarded as fair if the firms are different in some ways. If, for example, some of them could cut emissions at less cost, it might be regarded as more equitable to take this into account in the required cutbacks, or if some firms had already reduced emissions a lot while others hardly at all. This is a problem in international pollution control, where the issue is distributing a total reduction of CO_2 emissions, for example among countries.

Economists and others have done a lot of recent work on the relationship between environmental pollution and the distribution of income, particularly the unequal distribution of income. The effort includes studies from both directions: the influence of pollution on unequal income, and the influence of income inequality on the adoption of pollution-control policies. With the former the weight of the evidence is that factoring in ambient pollution levels makes the inequality of income more severe. And quality varies by region because of the location of primary sources. It disproportionately impacts households of lower income levels. Thus, if the monetized value of pollution damages is subtracted from nominal incomes it lowers the incomes of households of low income, and actually raises the income of households in the upper income brackets. Thus, diminished air quality actually makes the distribution of income more unequal.

Looked at from the other direction, there is some evidence that greater income inequality leads to higher levels of pollution. It has generally been thought that more wealthy countries would put greater effort into pollution control because all their basic needs have been met, so they should have better ambient conditions, other things equal. But there is some evidence that the relationship is weakened, or even reversed, by incomes that are more unequal.

Another issue, analogous to the abatement cost problem, arises because total damages are normally the aggregate of damages occurring in a number of different community groups. When we total the damages, do we treat all groups the same? Is a euro's worth of damages to a financially well-off group to be treated the same as a euro's worth of damages to a group of people with low or modest incomes? Economics has no way of answering this question. The best that can be said is that it is important for policy decision makers to have information on how the benefits and costs of pollution-control emissions are distributed among different groups within society.

The long run

We see that with the abatement cost and damage functions as pictured in Figure 3.1, efficient pollution control involves finding the emission level where the two factors intersect. This is a short-run, or static, analysis, where we are looking to balance or trade-off the factors involved. It takes as given the currently available pollution-control technology. It also takes as given the attitude that people have about living in a polluted natural environment. But in the long run, these underlying factors change.

Graphically, the appearance of new technology can be pictured as shifting the abatement cost function downward, for example to the dotted line (MAC_L) in Figure 3.1. This moves e*, the efficient level of emissions, downward. This change accords with common sense: the less expensive pollution control is, the more we would want. In some cases, like threats to the global climate, the future survival of something like present human societies is going to depend on the appearance of new pollution-control technologies. So we need to discuss the concepts and forces associated with the invention, development, and adoption of new pollution-control technology. This we will do in Chapter 4.

The other important long-run factor is change in damages. Upward shifts in MD move e* to the left, again an intuitive change: higher damage levels lower the socially efficient level of emissions, or ambient pollution levels. Higher damages come about in a number of ways. Population growth puts more people in the way of pollution, especially air pollution. The greater the exposure the greater the impacts, in health and other dimensions, for example, visibility.

Higher incomes may also shift the marginal damage function, depending on how one defines damage. If the value of damages is defined as what people would be willing to sacrifice to have the pollutants removed, then higher income will imply higher damages. As a person's income increases, so does their demand to live and work in an unpolluted environment. But "willingness to sacrifice" is obviously constrained by "ability to sacrifice," so by that standard people with low or moderate income would score low on damages associated with a polluted environment. The ethics of this are dubious.

Another factor that would raise MD is more widespread and more scientifically established information about the ill effects of certain pollutants. Substances that have been around for a long time may have been slow to have had effects on health: asbestos, for example. Newly introduced substances may have effects that are not understood: products of nanotechnology, for example. In these cases, the great public availability of knowledge can shift marginal damage relationships.

Lastly, people's attitudes toward risk may change. Environmental pollutants may have their effects probabilistically, they expose people to certain levels of risk, especially risk of health consequences. And environmental accidents, with their attendant consequences, expose people to the risk of damages. In this case "damages" must incorporate some notion of peoples' attitude toward risk, which may change over time. Although most of our discussion of damage is people-based, damage to ecosystems and to nonhuman living organisms is part of the mix.

Further reading

Boyce, J.K., K. Zwicki, and M. Ash (2015), *Three Measures of Environmental Inequality*, Political Economy Research Institute, Amherst, MA, Working Paper Series, No. 378.

Jha, A., P.H. Matthews, and N.Z. Muller (2019), "Does environmental Policy Affect Income Inequality? Evidence from the Clean Air Act," *AEA Papers and Proceedings*, Volume 109, pp. 271–276.

Johnstone, N. and J. Labonne (2006), "Environmental Policy, Management, and R&D," *OECD Economic Studies*, Number 42, Issue 1.

Muller, N.Z., P.H. Matthews, and V. Wiltshire-Gordon (2018), "The Distribution of Income is Worse Than You Think: Including Pollution Impacts into Measures of Income Inequality," *PLoS ONE*, Volume 13, Number 3, p. e0192461.

4 Technological change in pollution control

ESSENTIAL SUMMARY

We have described pollution-control decisions as involving a trade-off, of abatement costs and pollution damages. This is a short-run perspective, focusing on currently available technical options. In the long run, sustainability requires the transformation of the technologies of pollution control. The most straightforward interpretation of technical change is a shift back and down of the marginal abatement cost function. This implies technological innovations, the discovery and widespread adoption of new technologies that are more cost-effective than those available today. Of special importance is the connection between research and development (R&D) efforts and pollution-control regulations. Do pollution-control policies and regulations create strong incentives for pollution-control R&D, and for widespread adoption of new technologies?

The discussion in the last chapter focused on achieving better pollution control within the context of currently available technologies. But it is also clear that long-run goals of sustainability in pollution control, especially the response to global climate change, will need new and better technologies for reducing greenhouse gases. In this chapter, we discuss some of the leading ideas of this work.

Technological change: general issues

The simplest way to depict technological change in pollution control is as a shift to the left of the abatement cost function. Refer to Figure 3.1. Thus, for a given level of emissions, the marginal abatement cost is lowered, or, to say the same thing, a given marginal abatement cost is now associated with a lower emission level. The relationship could also change in other

DOI: 10.4324/9781003143635-4

ways, for example, MAC becoming less or more steep. This shift is the very simple depiction of something that could take many forms: a new way of treating the emissions stream; a change in output to reduce the emissions stream; a new system for recycling certain emissions; and so on. That doesn't necessarily mean that there will always be a clear association of R&D and abatement cost. Other reasons for innovation exist, for example to lower the chances of being found out of compliance.

It is useful to take a more disaggregate look at the production-pollution process, to identify the main pressure points where pollution control takes place. This is illustrated in Figure 4.1.

In the early days of pollution control, stress was put on the link between emissions and damages. This was called "end-of-pipe" technology, the treatment of emission streams to make them less damaging. For example, the timing of residual discharge could be changed, or the location. Or new technology could be developed, such as secondary and tertiary processes for treating domestic sewage, or taller smokestacks to distribute airborne pollutants more widely. Technology-based effluent standards were aimed primarily at the technology of emission treatment. And treatment technologies were linked to the different environmental media: land, air, and water.

Early emphasis was placed on recycling, so much so that the supply and demand imbalances for recycled materials were common. More recently, attention has been put on reducing the waste stream from production and consumption, so that it reduces the quantities of leftovers needing treatment or other forms of disposal. This has come to be called "waste reduction." It goes back to the first steps, such as the design of the good or service being produced, and the analyses of inputs, virgin and recycled, going into that production. End-of-pipe regulations put more emphasis on regulators becoming knowledgeable about available technologies. Changes in waste-reduction technology demand more on producers having the incentives for identifying and adopting innovative technologies and practices.

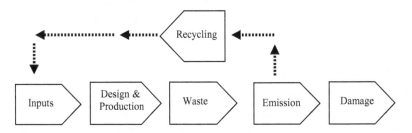

Figure 4.1 Production-pollution process

Technical innovation may be possible in some cases to reverse the emissions–damage link. In efforts to reduce climate change, technology is being explored that would pull carbon back out of the atmosphere. In early water-pollution control efforts, some attention was given to steps that would augment characteristics of water courses to make them better able to degrade certain pollutants. Soil rehabilitation may be possible in some cases to undo the buildup of certain contaminants.

The first prominent economist to think deeply about technological change was Joseph Schumpeter. He argued that technological innovation is central to capitalism, and the search for temporary profits arising from technological innovation was the driving force of entrepreneurship. Economists, and others, have argued over the essence and implications of his work. What is useful for our purposes is the idea that technological change can be divided into several steps, notably (1) invention, (2) innovation, and (3) adoption (diffusion). These are somewhat self-explanatory. Invention is the effect of basic research, to identify new technological means for dealing with environmental pollution. Innovation means incorporating these ideas into real-world technology that has improved results in terms of costs and pollution performance. Adoption refers to the spread of the technique from early adoptions to an entire industry.

Another way to think of these steps in technological change is basic research that looks for new and unique ideas, applied research that looks to incorporate the new ideas into practical technologies, and adoption decisions that determine how fast new technologies spread within polluting industries and among consumers. The first two of these come under the heading of research and development (R&D), in Europe called research and technological development (RTD).

A note of caution is in order, however. It is all well and good to search for, and plan for, future technologies that will seemingly solve our pollution-control problems. But just as critical is the need for the sensitivities and decisions of current generations to be attuned to the day-by-day needs of more and better pollution control. What this means in economic terms is the need to "get the prices right" today, i.e., to have markets and prices that truly reflect the social costs of environmental pollution and the social benefits of its reduction.

The economics of R&D

We discussed earlier the idea that environmental damages stem from market externalities: social spillover effects of private decisions. There is another important externality in the case of R&D. The information derived from R&D activity is essentially a public good. It can be made available to one firm or individual without diminishing its usefulness to others. The essential result of this is that the private return from doing R&D is lower than the full returns to society. Economists studying the returns to business from R&D and innovation consistently find that the returns to society are higher than the private rates of return to the firms doing the R&D. There is some evidence that this discrepancy is larger in environmental R&D than in general technology R&D.

In the real world, costs and benefits are highly uncertain; however, we represent the situation with a simple graph to explore its underlying economic logic. The situation is depicted in Figure 4.2. The curves show the private and social benefits from R&D conducted by firms in a given industry. The contours of the industry are somewhat ambiguous because R&D relevant to a part of the pollution-control process may be conducted by firms who are responsible for the pollution, or by firms that specialize in R&D itself. The private optimal level of R&D for the industry is r_1. From society's point of view, a higher level of R&D effort is optimal, r_2, because the total value includes the private value plus the external public values. This is a theoretical demonstration of why, in the real world, R&D efforts are likely to be less than the socially optimal level. This is sometimes called the "appropriability problem," a weaker incentive to do R&D because a substantial part of its benefits accrues to somebody other than the people doing the R&D. The relevant question is, what steps society should take to incentivize environmental R&D efforts.

One approach is to have a legal means of privatizing the technical information that the R&D produces. The classic way to do this is through

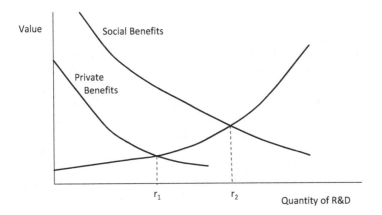

Figure 4.2 Knowledge externalities and the optimal level of environmental R&D

the public issuance and enforcement of patents. A patent gives the innovator an exclusive right to a technical procedure or process for a given period of time, and therefore the right to license it to buyers without losing control. For example, in the US, the patent for the original three-way catalytic converter for cars was awarded to John J. Mooney in the early 1970s. Patent laws are ubiquitous and can be controversial. One issue is how many years they should be in effect. Another is the international recognition of national patent laws. Although pollution-control patents are issued around the world, about 90 percent of them are done in the EU, the US, Japan, and Germany. Patents used to be primarily focused on machines, industrial processes, and articles of manufacture. But the development of the digital economy has extended patents to software and other information technologies.

In addition to the public goods nature of new technical knowledge, there are a number of other factors that make private pollution-control R&D suboptimal. First and foremost is that pollution control efforts are not profit driven in the traditional sense. They are usually regulation driven, either directly because of an explicit regulation or because of the prospects of future regulation. This increases the risk associated with private pollution-control R&D. While all investment has risk to some extent, pollution-control technology may be particularly risky when one considers both the evolution of the regulatory environment and changing public attitudes about the nature and the role of pollution control. It needs to be kept in mind that there is always another activity on which to spend R&D money: on efforts to cancel or weaken environmental regulations.

An obvious reaction to the information externality issue is public support of R&D. One way of doing this is to fund R&D programs within agencies of the public sector. Most countries have public research agencies whose mission is to conduct environmental R&D. A potential issue here is that R&D within the public sector may be more prone to political influence than activity in the private sector. The downside of political control was demonstrated when the US Environmental Protection Agency's R&D budget was drastically reduced by the incoming U.S. administration in 2017, which worked actively to reduce environmental regulation. Public R&D may be controversial because of the high risk sometimes involved. There can be political blowback from expensive research projects that do not develop successfully. The nuclear-breeder reactor debate in the US is an example.

Another approach to increasing effort in environmental R&D is public subsidies of private activity. This can be done with direct subsidies or with R&D focused fiscal incentives, such as tax incentives for R&D work. Public subsidies for R&D are common. Subsidies are a much easier political sell than is aggressive regulatory action. Much recent work has gone into determining whether R&D subsidies actually produce higher levels of R&D among targeted industries. The counter hypothesis is that publicly supported R&D "crowds outs" privately financed R&D. A number of papers have concluded that subsidized R&D supported through tax codes, leads to increased overall R&D efforts. Analysis of public environmental R&D subsidies suggests, however, that social welfare is much more likely to be enhanced by policies that directly affect the market externalities of environmental pollution.

A major question in the economics of environmental R&D is whether successful innovation in pollution-control technology is systematically related to the types of environmental policies and regulations that may be pursued. Historically, economists have argued that incentive-based policy approaches would lead to greater innovation than command-and-control regulations. Incentive-based policies provide financial rewards for innovation, while command-and-control regulations penalize firms that do not meet the standard and do not reward them for going further than the standard. Command-and-control policies are called that because they specify actions to be taken by polluters. Technology standards require polluters to adopt certain types of pollution-control technologies, which weaken the incentive to discover more cost-effective ways of reducing emissions. Standards have normally been tied to the adoption of certain technologies. In the US these are called "technology-based effluent standards." So incentive-based policies, emission charges, and cap-and-trade programs should, theoretically, provide stronger incentives for pollution-control R&D since they do not constrain the search to known and narrow technological channels. On the other hand, command-and-control policies may be better able to address the situation where concurrent R&D in associated technologies is needed.

Another important factor in the incentive effect of policy is its stringency. By stringency we mean the amount of pollution control required by regulation, rather than the type of regulation being used. Does more stringent regulation produce more R&D activity and more willingness of polluters to innovate? Theoretically it would seem so. The tighter the regulations, the more polluters should want to find means to lower compliance costs. In fact, there is a name for this in the US; it is called "technology forcing." This is where regulations are put in place for future emissions reduction that would be too costly for current technology, with the expectation that R&D and future innovation will lower the cost of meeting them. The popularity of the idea of technology forcing stems from its apparent success in setting rigorous tailpipe standards in the US in the 1970s, which encouraged car companies, many of them reluctantly, to adopt catalytic converters. On the other hand, technology forcing for airbags was less successful due to effective lobbying by car companies.

Some degree of technology forcing is underway in cars and trucks. Several major car companies have announced that they will stop producing cars with internal combustion gas engines as of a future date. The expectation is that they will shift to cars with electric motors, but how the electricity is to be supplied is not settled. Thus the whole infrastructure needed to support electric vehicles is yet to be developed. There are ongoing questions about whether advances in pollution-control technology come from pollution-control R&D directly, or more from basic research in chemicals, materials science, and engineering.

Economics of adoption (diffusion)

Technological innovators will have little impact on environmental quality unless they are widely adopted by polluters. This applies both to individual consumers faced with buying low emission appliances or cars, and polluting firms striving for market success. Technological diffusion has been widely studied by economists, sociologists, engineers, and others. The standard diffusion model for consumers faced with a new product, is an S-shaped path of adoption, with slow and increasing rates at the beginning, trending into a mid-range where diffusion is rapid and widespread, then a final phase where the diffusion rate slows and eventually tails to essentially zero when everyone has made the transition. The S-shaped diffusion model is based on information flows; as adoption happens, public knowledge of the item becomes more widespread, which boosts the rate of adoption. Eventually, the rate of adoption (adoption per unit of time) diminishes as the number of non-adopters dwindles.

The S-shaped adoption pattern may not be a good fit for market-oriented firms adopting new pollution-control technology because here the role of regulations looms large. These adoptions are primarily conditional, depending on whether regulations are in effect or expected to become so in the near future. They are also related to how rigorous the enforcement is, or will be, and whether it will be "hard" or "soft." Hard enforcement is when there is a clearly detailed limit with assumed sanctions for going beyond the limit. Soft enforcement is where authorities work with violations to fashion ways of coming into compliance with minimal formal sanctions.

In the early days of pollution control (1970s and 1980s), regulatory initiatives in pollution control were often based on the idea of taking technology decisions out of the hands of the polluters and putting them into the hands of regulators. Where monitoring and measuring emissions were technically difficult, control of emissions per se was not practicable. Thus, regulations were often tied to the adoption of the "best available pollution-control technology," (BAT) or some analogous standard. In these cases, technology choices are basically set by pollution-control regulators, usually in collaboration with the polluting industry. In many parts of the world technology standards are still relied upon. There is a tension between the desire to have pollution control based on the specification of certain technologies and the need for these technologies to be economically viable. Thus in the US, for example, there were standards based on "best practicable technology," and, in other countries, "best available technology not entailing excessive costs," and "best practicable control technology." Technology specifications by regulators may appear to be straightforward and effective, and in many cases they are. But they also can have perverse incentives. Firms subject to technology standards may have little incentive to look for, and adopt, better technology, if it would precipitate regulatory actions against them. This happened in the US with its program of "new source review" for power plants. However, the concept of BAT is still used around the world, sometimes as a regulatory prescription and sometimes as an advisory standard. It is used particularly for hard to measure emissions, especially for the handling of chemicals. It is sometimes included in international environmental agreements, for example the Minamata Convention on Mercury adopted in 2017. Technology adoption issues have been more prominent as pollution control has swung more towards incentive-based regulations, and as better technologies for measuring emissions have become available.

Another quasi-regulatory approach, especially with non-point source pollutants, is "best management practices" (BMP). These are procedures and technologies (usually "low tech") that are known to deal effectively with these types of pollutants. BMPs are often advisory, and sometimes required by regulation. BMPs are especially frequent in agricultural operations, wastewater handling, wetlands management, and chemicals handling. They are used in conjunction with standard pollution-control regulations, and often subsidized by local or regional governments.

The adoption process can be looked at as a supply and demand phenomenon. Supply comes from the efforts of R&D firms to develop superior methods of pollution control; demand comes from the polluting firms, or individuals, whose emissions are subject to regulatory control or who wish to reduce their environmental footprints. On the demand side the predominant force behind adoption is regulatory pressure. The trade-off between environmental practices and profitability has been emphasized by many researchers. The willingness to adopt new technologies hinges on a cost-benefit type of analysis, comparing economic costs with the benefits of reducing regulatory pressure. However, customer pressure can move firms toward the adoption of environmentally friendly technology. It can even move firms beyond the point of strict compliance. One would expect that customer pressure and regulatory pressure would be mutually reinforcing.

It is clear that binding regulatory requirements can induce firms to adopt pollution-control technologies that they otherwise would not adopt. For the most part, studies conclude that incentive-based policies are effective in motivating the adoption of new technologies. Studies also seem to indicate that regulatory pressure is more likely to motivate end-of-pipe adoptions rather than internal process change.

While benefit-cost considerations are important in decisions to adopt new technologies, behavioral issues also appear to play a large part, not only for individual consumers choosing among products, but also for firms who presumably are searching for market success. This means behaviors that appear to be irrational on the surface may actually stem from persistent individual biases or understandings (often called "framings") of decision situations. One well-known example is consumers faced with choices to buy energy-efficient appliances. Studies have shown that many people will choose not to buy a higher cost, more energy-efficient appliance, even though the projected savings in energy costs over the life of the item are much greater than the initial cost. Economists have called this phenomenon the "energy-efficiency gap." Consumers put near-term cost minimization over long-term energy savings. Consumers may be using a higher-than-expected discount rate or placing a higher negative value on future risk. Behavioral economists stress the importance of seemingly irrational decisions made when consumers are faced with situations involving risk. Sometimes consumers react differently to a sales tax credit than to an income tax credit of the same value when considering the purchase of a hybrid fueled car. Analogous patterns have been found among firms faced with decisions to adopt a new pollution-control technology. They tend to put much more weight on the up-front capital costs of adoption rather than the annual savings the adoption will generate in the future.

Another important factor is the possible presence of what is called the rebound effect among consumers. It is easiest to see this with cars. New cars are being developed that get much better mileage per unit of fuel than existing ones. Better mileage implies that the costs per mile of travel will go down. But if this cost per mile goes down, a normal reaction of people will be to drive more. This works against – and offsets in whole or in part – the objective of the original change, which was to reduce fuel consumption.

In addition to behavioral issues of this type, there are other possible sources of a reluctance to adopt new technologies. Adoption of pollution-control technology can sometimes be hindered by the presence of network effects; these are when changes in one part of a system may require changes somewhere else in that system. A large-scale conversion to electric cars may require substantial changes in the transmission grid to match the electricity that will be needed. This is essentially a case of external benefits: earlier adoptions create more advantageous conditions for later adopters, through better information, or in complementary technical availabilities. Analogous effects could flow from highly integrated supply chains. Another problem on the demand side is capital market failures, which limit the supply of financial capital to innovating adopters.

If the adoption of environmental technologies is too slow from the perspective of society, what are the means for making it more rapid? Governments can encourage the adoption of new technologies through subsidies, like tax credits to adopters. Another is direct payments to cover the cost of new equipment. The politics of subsidies is very different from the politics of regulation and can be problematic in at least two senses. First, a lot of the adoption may have occurred without subsidies, but there is no effective way of knowing which ones. Second, many of the subsidies may end up in the bank accounts of technology suppliers, through price increases, and not in those of the adopters themselves.

A major source for strengthening the demand side of the adoption market is public procurement, the actual purchase and use of new technologies by government agencies, such as the purchase of hybrid buses by public transportation agencies. Public procurement of "greener" technology helps overcome information availability problems by giving an assured market to more environmentally friendly technologies and outputs. Procurement can be focused on existing products and technologies, or on innovative technologies.

A short-run analysis of pollution control, featuring a trade-off between damages and abatement costs, should be augmented by a long-run perspective, in which change in pollution-control technology becomes an important force. Critical to this is a better understanding of the interplay between regulation and the incentives for technical innovation and adoption.

Further reading

Acemoglu, D., et al. (2012), "The Environment and Directed Technological Change," *American Economic Review*, Volume 102, Number 1, pp. 131–166.

Ghisetti, C. (2017), "Demand-Pull and Environmental Innovations: Estimating the Effects of Public Procurement," *Technology Forecasting, and Social Change*, Volume 125, pp. 178–187.

Popp, D., R.G. Newell, and A.B. Jaffe (2009), *Energy, Environment, and Technological Change*, National Bureau of Economic Research, Working Paper 14832, Cambridge, MA.

Yalabik, B. and R.J. Fairchild (2011), "Customer Regulatory and Competitive Pressure as Drivers of Environmental Innovation," *International Journal of Production Economies*, Volume 131, pp. 519–527.

5 Measuring the benefits and costs of pollution control

ESSENTIAL SUMMARY

If concepts such as pollution damages and abatement costs are to have more than theoretical significance, we must be able to actually measure them. When discussing pollution-control policy it is important to know, and to be able to compare, the benefits and costs of pollution control regulations. The benefits are the reductions in pollution damages they bring about. The costs are the value of resources devoted to this activity rather than to something else. The benefits of pollution damage reduction are usually greater than the direct impacts of pollution on health because they are related to the value people place on living and working in a less polluted environment. This chapter covers the methods economists have developed to measure these values. It covers some of the issues involved in that work, such as discounting future values, and the value of risk reduction.

In the previous chapter, we set up a "model" to depict how we can understand the short-run and long-run interactions of pollution damage reduction and abatement costs. In later chapters, we will use that model to explore the actions that can be taken to reduce pollution. However, if the notion of abatement costs and damages is to have anything more than theoretical existence, we need to find ways of actually measuring them in comprehensible ways.

The damage and abatement cost evaluations fit naturally within the framework of what is called "benefit-cost analysis," a common type of analysis used often to evaluate public programs, such as regulatory initiatives to combat environmental pollution.

DOI: 10.4324/9781003143635-5

Benefit-cost analysis

Benefit-cost analysis is a method of estimating the social benefit and social costs associated with public initiatives. In the private sector, individual firms often depend on revenue and cost analyses to assess the feasibility of actions. Most environmental protection efforts, on the other hand, involve public action, where revenues are not as relevant. Hence the notion of a technique that involves comparing the social benefits of programs with their social costs: benefit-cost analysis. Benefit-cost analysis is to public agencies what revenue-cost analysis is to private firms. It requires, first, that programs be described in detail, in terms of the inputs required and the output expected. It then involves expressing these inputs and outputs in value terms, using whatever monetary terms are relevant to the particular case. Then the results are presented, sometimes in terms of a benefit-cost ratio $\left(\dfrac{benefits}{costs} \right)$, or sometimes in terms of net benefits (*benefits – costs*).

Benefit-cost analysis can be controversial. Some think that the benefit of pollution control is too hard to measure since benefits don't move directly through markets with prices to indicate value. Some think that measuring the value of environmental protection will invariably come up with values that are too low, and therefore misleading. Or that costs will be measured with greater precision, and therefore be given added weight. Environmental policy is a politically contested process. Those who operate in this arena in the name of environmental protection will have more influence if they are able to present good quality estimates of the damages caused by pollution. Not just "air pollution is causing discomfort to people downwind," but "air pollution from those power plants is causing an estimated 5,000 excess deaths per year." And pollution-control policies adopted in the past can be defended better if they can be shown to have had a measurable effect on reducing pollution damages.

Pollution damage estimates can also facilitate green accounting. Green accounting is a procedure for incorporating the natural world into standard economic measures, like Gross Domestic Product (GDP). GDP and other measures are in monetary terms, so including nature means expressing in comparable value terms such things as natural resource depletion and environmental contamination. This means putting a value on environmental externalities.

The concept of sustainability also involves assessing the long-run implications of resource and environmental decisions taken today. Sustainability was originally expressed as meeting today's needs without compromising the ability of future generations to meet their own needs. Sustainability can be expressed in physical terms: maintaining the physical stock of a resource or maintaining the physical parameters of the environment. It may also be expressed in value terms, that is, maintaining the value of an environmental asset. This again brings up the valuation question.

Valuing the damages of pollution

The benefits of reducing pollution are the reduction in damages caused by the pollution. Measuring pollution damage involves the following steps:

1. Measuring emissions and the ambient quality of the affected environment.
2. Estimating the exposure and physical impacts of the polluted environment, both on humans and on other features of the biosphere.
3. Putting a value on the physical impacts.

The first two of the steps are normally done by physical and laboratory scientists, epidemiologists, and health scientists. The last step is the normal purview of economists.

Shapes of damage functions

We often use damage estimates made for discrete values of emissions and ambient conditions. These are helpful in environmental policy controversies. But even more useful is the knowledge of damage functions, showing how damages increase or decrease with changes in pollution levels. This is especially true when dealing with global climate change, in which damages are expected to increase over time.

Figure 5.1 shows several different shapes of damage functions. These can be understood as marginal damage functions, at any point they show how much damages would be changed if the ambient environmental quantity, however measured, changes by one unit. Damage functions must be understood to be time specific. They show emissions or ambient conditions for a specific time, likewise for damages. For a non-cumulative pollutant, the interpretation is straightforward: damages are effects that occur only in a certain time period. In other cases, they refer to damages that last over multiple time periods, such as health impacts. For a pollutant that accumulates over time, the damage function may relate to the cumulative value that people place on the aggregate of current and future damage impacts. In each of the illustrated cases, damages increase as the ambient content of a pollutant increases. Damage function A shows damage as a strictly

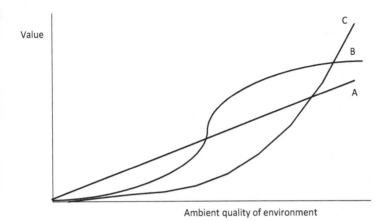

Figure 5.1 Possible pollution damage functions

linear response to diminished ambient quality. If the scales on both axes were linear, then the increase in damages would actually be declining in percentage terms. Function C shows a strictly convex function showing how damage increases more rapidly as the ambient condition changes. But this function shows a "threshold," a certain level of ambient quantity below which there are no damages. This may apply to radiation exposure, and exposure to small concentrations of some chemicals (health scientists often say, "It's the size of the dose that causes damage"). Damage function B begins at the origin, increases rapidly over a range, then less rapidly at higher levels of the pollutants.

While this may seem a topic of limited importance, it has actually led to vigorous controversies in the policy world where pollution-control standards are set. Many such standards are written for and set at levels below which damages are assumed to be in some sense minimal. For many circumstances that minimum is controversial, such as with chemical exposure and noise.

Direct damage valuation

Some environmental changes have direct impacts on health factors or other economic outcomes, with costs that can be measured directly. Air pollution is linked to increases in such things as asthma, bronchitis, and lung cancer. The cost-of-illness approach measures the direct costs of pollution-induced diseases, including the costs for hospitalization and other treatments, and direct effects in terms of lost productivity and lost incomes of the affected people. An analogous type of approach is the lost agricultural production and income that results from air or water pollution. In this case, decreased crop yields can be assessed and valued according to the relevant market prices of the crops involved.

The basic problem with direct measures is that they are usually incomplete. Valuing the health impact on children is a good case in point. They are not in the job market, so their health changes can't be measured via income changes. Even for adults these direct effects may be incomplete. If I catch a cold, it might affect me directly through the cost of a bottle of aspirin I use to feel better. But the value to me of avoiding the cold, if I could, would be more than the cost of the bottle of aspirin. Hence the value of avoiding a pollution-related health condition is likely to be more than just the avoided costs of health care.

Indirect damage valuation

For these reasons, environmental economists have used several indirect means to measure environmental externalities. Indirect studies require that the quantity of something for which we know the value (in this case the price) be correlated with the environmental feature whose value we wish to measure. One of these approaches is "averting costs." People will sometimes take steps to avert, or avoid, adverse environmental conditions. Noise around airports or near major roads can be avoided somewhat by putting in more home insulation or double-thick window-panes. Contaminated water can be avoided by installing water treatment devices. Averting costs also are likely to be an underestimate of true externality damages. However, they do focus on one thing: the willingness of people to take specific steps to avoid environmental pollution. This notion of "willingness to sacrifice" has become a leading way to think about environmental damages. That is, damages of pollution can be best thought of, and measured by, the willingness of people to incur costs to avoid the damage of pollution. Thus this willingness to sacrifice, or incur costs, is the basic concept economists use to measure the damages of pollution. This is misunderstood to be a concept that is relevant only in economies with money, but it is applicable to all economies, including barter economies, and economic decisions by hermits.

Willingness to pay vs. ability to pay

The ability to pay is a function of the distribution of income. This is a public good, and the result in part of the collective behavior of the people in the group. The willingness to pay for environmental improvement by a low-income group is an understatement of the collective willingness to pay for that improvement because income constrains the willingness to pay of that group. And the willingness to pay for a high-income group is an overstatement of the collective willingness to pay for that group. In practical terms, it means that willingness to pay estimates for people within one income group should not be compared to the willingness to pay estimates of people in another income group.

Willingness to pay: indirect measures

Suppose in a small city there is a fossil-fueled power plant whose smoke emissions deteriorate air quality in the northern, but not the southern, part of the city. We get data on historic air quality indices throughout the city. We also study real-estate data to get historical records of house prices as homes have been bought and sold over time. We then examine the differences in prices between houses in the north and houses in the south of the city. We have to be careful because lots of factors affect house prices: size, commuting distance from town, local amenities, etc. We then find, through statistical analysis, that houses in the smoky part of town sold, on average, for a lower price than those in the clean-air part of town. We can interpret the price difference as a measure of what people were willing to pay for cleaner air. Or, what is the same thing, how much homeowners are made worse off (damaged) by the air pollution. This is called an indirect measure because it measures the value of an environmental amenity by evaluating the impact on the price of something that is correlated with the amenity. We might use a similar method to estimate the values people place on living next to open space, or the value people have for living in a less noisy neighborhood, or the value that people have for living near a lake with fine water quality, or for living in a flood-prone area. And knowing these values would give us a way of estimating the damages people would experience if their environments became more heavily polluted.

Value of a statistical life (VSL)

A 2019 study in the US concluded that fine particulate air pollution in the US is responsible for about 105,000 premature deaths per year. A premature death is a death that occurs before the expected life span of the individual in question. For many, numbers like this are a clarion call for devoting more resources to pollution control. For them any attempt to convert this into a monetary value of damages is superfluous. But for environment protection agencies involved in pollution control politics it is not. If they spend a billion more dollars, or euros, on air pollution control, will the benefits, in terms of reduced damage, be worth it?

Questions like these have led economists to develop an estimate for the "value of a statistical life" (VSL) that may be used in evaluating environmental policies. This concept stems from the idea that risk reduction has a value. Risk refers to the general probability of an event, or its occurrence, on a random basis, rather than to any specifically named individual. The risk in this case is the risk of premature death.

People living with polluted air will actively have a higher risk, i.e., the probability of contracting a disease such as lung cancer or acute bronchitis. Cleaning up the air will lower this probability. Suppose that we do a sample survey and find that for a group of 100,000 people, the average person would be willing to pay $20 to lower the probability of illness or premature death within this group from 7 in 100,000 to 6 in 100,000. Then the total willingness to pay is $20 x 100,000 or $2,000,000 which is the VSL in this situation for this group.

How to get a realistic estimate of the VSL? The approach has been to assess the amounts people will pay, or accept, for situations involving different amounts of risk. Studies have been done, for example, of wage differentials among jobs that have different risk levels, such as, construction work versus office work. Studies have shown that the average VSL in the United States was about $10 million in 2017. It is somewhat lower in other countries, reflecting the fact that on a national level it is correlated with income level. Studies in other OECD countries have found somewhat lower values ($2–3 million, for example).

Direct valuation methods

In a direct approach, respondents are asked directly to express a value for an environmental feature. This most common direct approach is called "contingent valuation" because respondents are asked to express a value for a "what if" or contingent situation. This method was first applied to natural resource features, e.g., the value of having access to a wilderness reservation area. Now it is used also to obtain values for features of environmental quality. For example, water quality in a nearby river or stream, improved air quality from air pollution reduction, or reduced noise levels from passing traffic. In a contingent valuation study, researchers devise and administer surveys with willingness-to-pay types of questions. For example, "how much would you be willing to pay to have the air quality in your neighborhood improved by x percent?" Contingent valuation techniques have been applied to the problem of valuing health conditions, for example, people's willingness to pay to avoid certain conditions of ill health. Contingent valuation is used to get estimates of VSL, by asking questions about willingness to pay to lower the probability of premature death.

Elaborate techniques have been developed by researchers to frame questions and to administer surveys in ways that will elicit truthful responses.

Although contingent valuation is well established, it is well known that attitude surveys are vulnerable to outcomes in which answers depend on how questions are worded. Asking respondents to evaluate hypothetical situations may yield results that offer hypothetical answers. And questions have arisen as to whether respondents are answering strategically, with the intention of inflating the value of an environmental feature for which they have a special regard. On the other hand, the strength of the approach is that it can be used to value environmental features that are not directly transacted in a regular marketplace. It is sometimes called a stated preference method, since it relies on respondents making explicit statements about their values (their willingness to pay) for particular environmental features.

Measuring costs

The other half of environmental benefit-cost analysis is the cost of the projects or programs being evaluated. The importance of costs is obvious from our previous analysis. The lower the costs, i.e., the lower the abatement cost function, the lower the efficient level of pollution and the greater the amount of pollution control society should seek. Conversely, the higher the cost, the less the socially efficient level of pollution control. This makes cost estimation a controversial activity. It is routine for regulated industries to argue that the expected costs of pollution-control plans will adversely affect them and the economy, especially employment levels. The environmental community maintains the opposite. When the regulation being evaluated is one applicable to a single plant, or a single industry, the most likely source of cost data is the regulated industries themselves. This creates an information asymmetry, with the regulated entities often having a much better sense of what their costs are, or will be, than the regulators or policy makers. The history of pollution-control policy is replete with cases where pollution-control targets have been achieved at costs lower than initially predicted by the regulated firms. This is a main reason why environmental economists have stressed the value of incentive-base regulations. It sets targets but leaves polluters latitude to find the least costly way of reaching them.

An absolutely critical factor on the cost side is how future changes in technology will affect future control costs. Technological change, the invention and application of new and better pollution-control technologies, is usually hard to predict. We know it will occur, but at what rate? Controversies in current environmental policy often hinge on differences of opinion about what pollution abatement costs will be in the future as a result of the development and adoption of new technologies. In the United States, a concept that has been used occasionally by regulators is "technology forcing." This means setting a pollution-control target that is overly costly with today's technology, yet feasible if polluters develop new, lower cost, technologies. The aim is to create the incentive for more pollution-control research and development for lower cost technology.

Who pays for the cost increases is also a matter of concern. Firms whose costs increase will normally try to pass on that increase in the form of higher prices to consumers for their output. This cost pass-through depends on the state of competition in the industry, as we will discuss in Chapter 8. A matter of importance is the incidence of costs, or who actually ends up paying the costs. If it is a public program, such as a subsidy for reducing emissions, the cost will be borne by taxpayers. If it is a regulatory program aimed at reducing emissions from firms in a competitive industry, the costs may be passed along to buyers in the form of higher prices. Under conditions of monopoly or oligopoly, some of the costs will be borne by the owners of the firms in the form of lower net income.

Discounting

Benefit-cost analysis was first widely used in the 1950s in the US to evaluate the feasibility of federally built flood-control dams. With this kind of facility, the costs, mostly construction costs, were experienced early in the dam's life while the benefits accumulated gradually over the life of the dam. This is not unlike programs of pollution control. Costs are often incurred in the near term. Pollution-control equipment is installed today, the benefits of which will occur through time. Solar-power generation involves up-front costs and future benefits. Water-treatment plants are built today and utilized by future generations. Steps can be taken today to reduce emissions of greenhouse gases. The benefits will accrue largely to future generations. The question is how we compare values that occur at different points of time. The answer has been by discounting future values back to the present.

Discounting is the reverse of compounding. If you put M euros in the bank at five percent, it will be worth $M(1 + .05)$ euros after one year, assuming simple compounding. We can write this as $M_F = M_P(1+.05)$ or, in general terms, $M_F = M_P(1+r)$, where M_F is the future value, M_p is the present value, and r is the interest rate. In reverse, a sum that will be received next year has a present value of $M_P = M_F(1+r)^{-1}$. Thus discounting establishes the present value of future amounts, which now gives us a way of evaluating amounts realized in different years; we can do it in terms of their present values. This represents the way a rational person behaves. When somebody deposits a sum in a bank at a certain interest rate, they are demonstrating a willingness to forego a value today for a future compounded value. This apparently stems from the fact that most people are short sighted to a certain extent, both because all humans are finite in age, and because they are to some extent psychologically near sighted.

The other factor behind discounting is that acting in the present has opportunity costs. Devoting resources to a project today foregoes the return these resources would have earned if they instead had been invested in a growing economy. If it is normally expected that the rate of return on standard investments averages, say, six percent, this is the return that decision makers will be foregoing if they instead use resources in a current project. To account for this, the future benefits of the project can be discounted back to present values at the ongoing rate of return. Thus these future values (the benefits of a project or program) are discounted back to the present to allow for the foregone opportunity of putting resources into alternative investments. When future values (benefits or costs) are discounted it tends to privilege near-term costs over long-run benefits. But discounting appears to run counter to notions of sustainability. Discussions of sustainability sometimes proceed without a definite notion of what it is that is being sustained. At the very least, however, it is an idea, or a felt inclination, that decisions of today ought to be made with reference to their long-run implications. Discounting greatly influences the analysis of global climate change. Briefly, the question at issue today is how much to spend now to reduce the future damages of climate change. Future damages are probabilistic and could be very high. If we do not discount future benefits, we give them greater weight when comparing them with current costs; therefore, this encourages higher levels of spending now to reduce emissions.

If future benefits are discounted, then the apparent benefits of controlling emissions now are reduced. This trade-off is key to setting global climate change policy.

Further reading

Carson, Richard (2012), "Contingent Valuation: A Practical Attention When Prices Aren't Available," *Journal of Economic Perspectives*, Volume 24, Number 4, pp. 27–42.

Muller, N.Z. and R.O. Mendelsohn (2007), "Measuring the Damages Due to Air Pollution in the United States," *Journal of Environmental Economics and Management*, Volume 54, pp. 1–14.

Navrud, Stals (2018), *Assessing the Economic Valuation of the Benefits of Regulating Chemicals, Lessons Learned from Five Case Studies*, OECD Working Paper 136, OECD Publishing, Paris.

OECD (2018), *Cost Benefit Analysis and the Environment Further Development and Policy Use*, OECD Publishing, Paris.

Viscusi, W.K. (2018), *Pricing Lives: Guideposts for a Safer Society*, Princeton University Press, Princeton, NJ.

6   The policy world

ESSENTIAL SUMMARY

Environmental pollution comes from externalities: environmental impacts that spill over from private transactions in markets or elsewhere. The extent of these externalities, and the ways they can be addressed and rectified, are critically affected by the law and policy institutions that can be called into play at different levels of public action. At the local level, collective action involves just an adjustment among neighbors, or community committees that can work informally. At a higher level, it involves the actions of groups at the regional or national level, working through governance institutions that promulgate and enforce regulations at this level. The effectiveness of national policies can be evaluated using a number of criteria. Beyond the national level we are in the realm of international affairs, where collective action requires that sovereign nations find a way to address externalities running across national borders. In this chapter, we will briefly review some of the factors that are at work at different levels of public actions where environmental economics runs into environmental policy.

The local level

By "local level" we mean the level of individual towns and communities where environmental externalities stem from local actions, and damages are confined to local individuals or groups. Perhaps the first thought here is the possible role of voluntary action as an alternative to public regulation. Communities, and countries, have often encouraged voluntary action, especially in cases where "emissions" are dispersed and hard to monitor. Litter

DOI: 10.4324/9781003143635-6

control is one example. Laws against littering may be enacted yet getting people to behave accordingly may best be encouraged by public pronouncements and appeals to conscience. Voluntary efforts to recycle may also be encouraged by public announcements, the public availability of receptacles, and simple pressure that people can exert on friends and neighbors. This is moral pressure, and it undoubtedly can work locally to some extent in getting individuals to reduce their pollution footprints.

Consider, for example, the case of a small lake, where around the shores a dozen homeowners live who use the lake as a repository for household sewage. The homeowners meet and agree that each of them will install a new septic system to reduce their emissions. With no formal monitoring and enforcement, attaining compliance must come from either the moral attitudes of individuals or from social pressure, with neighbors essentially monitoring and sanctioning one another through informal means.

When the relevant community has a large population, and personal connections among its members are tenuous, the community may be less able to generate enough social pressure to obtain significant emissions reductions. In this case, voluntarism can work through the formation of organizations that take it upon themselves, with or without a public mandate, to protect their environmental resources. The formation of organizations to control access to a valuable natural resource has been much studied, particularly by Nobel Laureate Elinor Ostrom and people who have carried on her work.

Suppose, in the lake example, rather than the pollution coming from the homeowners, the pollution comes from a single plant that discharges wastewater into the lake. Social pressure alone may be insufficient to resolve the pollution-control problem. Communities sometimes have power sufficient to implement pollution-control regulations. When that happens there is some degree of confidence that the community itself will find its own level of e*, the level of emissions that is efficient and equitable from its own perspective. In many countries, however, pollution control is centralized, meaning that upper-level agencies have the power to set pollution-control procedures. In this case, regulatory actions taken by the state can frequently conflict with the desires of local groups.

In economics, the school of thought known as "law and economics" has stressed the importance of laws establishing explicit property rights over the resource in question, in this example the waters of the lake. Ownership could be held either by the residents around the lake, or by the owner(s) of the polluting plant. There is a famous theorem in property rights economics asserting that negotiations among the affected parties can reach e*, the socially optimal level of plant emissions, no matter who has the property rights over the lake waters. If the plant is the owner, the homeowners can compensate the plant for the cost of cutting back its emissions. If the waters are owned by the homeowners, the plant can compensate them for the right to emit wastewater into the lake.

Theoretically, if negotiations could be initiated by either party, and if they could proceed without bias and with roughly equal bargaining strength, they could arrive at e*, or close to it. Although the direction of compensation runs in the opposite direction for the two cases, generalizing this kind of procedure to much larger cases of industrial pollution, with multiple pollution sources and thousands of people experiencing damages, seems unrealistic. In particular, one could not expect the parties to have roughly equal bargaining power, so it would make a difference as to which party had the initial right to use the water in the lake. Still, it may be relevant to cases where there is a small number of polluters, and a small neighborhood of people being damaged.

Central to any kind of voluntary action is the information that is available about people's exposure to environmental risks. If people do not know what pollutants are in the water they drink or in the air they breathe, there is no way for a voluntary effort to get organized. This is the justification for laws, called the Pollution Release and Transfer Register or "sunshine laws" in many countries, that require firms to make known publicly their toxic emissions and other details of their toxics handling operations. The theory is that if the information becomes public, the people affected will, or can, bring public pressure to bear on firms to reduce their emissions, or to reduce the threat of accidental releases.

How effective they are is another question. People, in general, are not good at assessing risk. In recent years, behavioral economics has brought certain psychological insights about people's choice behavior into decision situations they face. One underlying notion is that individuals may sometimes make choices that seem on the surface to be irrational. Behavioral economics is behind what is called "nudge theory." A nudge is an informal hint or clue that helps resolve ambiguity and push decisions in one way or another. For example, electricity consumers can be supplied with data on the electricity consumption of "efficient neighbors," on the theory that they would be influenced, by a sort of social pressure, to reduce their own consumption to match or better that of their neighbors. While nudges are interesting and sometimes surprising, it's debatable whether they could be used to make a big dent in industrial-scale pollution with multiple sources and widespread damage.

Another form of volunteerism is from private firms, or individuals, to announce certain pollution-control goals or procedures, but with no legal directive or formal regulation to ensure compliance. Voluntarily announced goals to reduce carbon footprints, for example, are common, as are agreements to conduct environmental audits. Such efforts are often described as "green washing" because they can give the impression of environmental activities without any assurance of compliance. Experience has shown that compliance in these cases depends heavily on there being a credible threat of public regulation if goals are not met voluntarily.

One important pollution issue that has devolved to local communities is the management of household trash, normally termed municipal solid waste (MSW), or simply municipal waste. MSW requires systems, sometimes large systems, for collection and transport. MSW that is not recycled or composted (for organic material) or incinerated for energy production goes to a landfill.

Communities around the world have sought in many ways to reduce and manage the growing quantities of MSW. Some are based on reducing the flow of MSW that has to be disposed of, such as product bans and "pay-as-you-throw" systems. Some are based on finding new directions for the material, such as energy recovery. And there has been a major effort given to recycling. Recycling ranges from simple acts (giving an unwanted tool or piece of furniture to a neighbor) to a complex sequence involving collection reprocessing, redistribution, and reuse.

The need for recycling depends in part on the materials intensity of production. The lower the intensity the lower the demand for materials, including recycled materials. In the short run, the efficient level of recycling is a balance between its benefits and its costs. Recycling reduces the amount of waste that flows back into the environment. But recycling is not costless. We would expect that the marginal cost of recycling would increase as the recycling ratio (in this case the proportion of materials used that are recycled) increases. As the recycling ratio increases, the marginal benefits of further recycling diminish. Where marginal recycling costs equal marginal recycling benefits is the socially efficient recycling ratio. This clearly depends on the type of material involved (plastic, wood, metals). It also depends on political factors since there is great variation in national recycling ratios.

Many programs have been put in place to try and increase recycling ratios. Again, we can think of this as a question of supply and demand. Demand refers to the willingness of firms to accept quantities of recycled material, do whatever reprocessing is necessary, and then make it available for reuse. Demand depends on standard market factors: projections of future prices, the technical ability to collect and transport recycled materials, willingness to invest in the necessary processing facilities, and assurance of supply. This is a subject where developments in national and international recycled materials markets have impinged on local recycling practices. Efforts by countries to encourage, or discourage, international trade in recycles can be felt at local levels by an increase or decrease in the revenues they can obtain from recycled materials.

State, region, and country level

Many years ago pollution problems were dealt with mostly at the local level. But in the present day, it is clear that the most active and consequential efforts to control environmental pollution are at the country level, or in some cases the provincial or state level. This is where policy institutions and initiatives mainly exist for putting laws and regulations on the books, and more importantly for putting in place procedures for enforcing them.

Each country has its own distinct governance institutions, and a unique political culture that shapes the way policies are, or are not, mobilized to counter such social problems as environmental pollution. Many economists believe that there is a rough relationship between countries' economic development trajectories and their efforts to control pollution. When countries are focused on economic development, especially industrial development, they may not give priority to environmental pollution control. As economic security increases with development, people will demand an environment with less pollution, so political and policy institutions will act toward that end. It continues to be true, however, that typical policy institutions and policy processes will differ greatly among countries. Some of the differences are:

- The degree of openness to citizen participation in shaping and revising policies. This has been called environmental democracy.
- The fostering of technical and scientific expertise about matters such as the sources of pollution and the damages it causes.
- The willingness to set reasonably ambitious goals and put in place procedures for effective enforcement.
- The extent to which people will participate in international efforts, especially the effort to control global climate change.

There is a plethora of public policies and regulations actually or potentially available for pollution control. This is a good place to consider the criteria that can be used to sort out the best from the less good. Here are the most common criteria:

1. Cost-effectiveness: cost-effectiveness means getting the most pollution control for the resources spent. Alternatively, it can be phrased as obtaining the pollution control we want for the lowest possible social cost. It most emphatically does not mean minimizing pollution-control costs. Rather it is what in economics is called a "conditional minimization": given the level of pollution control desired (e.g., given the reduction in emissions sought), what is the minimum cost of achieving it?

2. Efficiency, more accurately called "social efficiency": this means getting the amount of pollution control that is "optimal" in the sense that it balances damages and abatement costs. If cost-effectiveness means maximizing pollution control from a given resource expenditure, efficiency means, in addition, reaching the socially optimal amount of pollution control.

3. Equity: equity means what is fair. A pollution-control policy that is equitable is one that affects people in different circumstances in ways that are deemed fair. These could include people in different income classes or people in predominantly minority or ethnic neighborhoods. Principles of environmental equity hold that the costs of pollution should not fall disproportionately on people who are in disadvantaged economic circumstances. In addition, net benefits (benefits minus costs) of pollution control should not disproportionately accrue to people in superior economic circumstances. Equity, or fairness, does not come with ready-made criteria for recognizing it or attaining it. But two things can be said about it. One is that environmental pollution-control policy is best not to be understood as welfare policy. Welfare policy is established to raise the economic circumstances of disadvantaged members of society. Another cogent dictum regarding fairness is that in pursuing any pollution-control policy, indeed in pursuing any type of policy, the people who are made worse off should be compensated for their loss.

4. Sustainability: this is a long-run criterion; by long run, we mean future generations, perhaps those of the distant future. Often it is not made clear exactly what is to be sustained over time. What is implied is a point of view that natural resources policy and pollution-control policy, or the lack of such policies, are too short sighted. To some extent this is a matter of attitudes. But there are several specific factors involved. One is the use of discount rates to evaluate the long-run consequences of policies. Another is the special attention that needs to be given to factors that will induce changes in the trade-off between pollution damages and abatement costs, especially to technical changes that will lower future abatement costs.

5. Enforceability: the world is littered with pollution-control programs and policies that are not sufficiently enforced or are too costly to enforce. Policies that require more or better data than are available, or require superabundant enforcement resources, are not likely to be effective.

6. Political acceptability: this would appear to be a non-economic criterion. In most countries, at least those where there is some degree of public participation in governmental decisions, the enactment and enforcement of environmental policies is usually a matter of conflict

and contention. There is often a disjunction between objectives, which sometimes are aspirational, and the regulations put in place to achieve them. It is an advantage when a proposed policy has enough political support to be put into effect and enforced. It is a disadvantage when a policy does not have that support. It is also true that policies need to be adjusted from time to time. Any pollution-control policy is better if modest adjustments to it can be made without precipitating huge political or administrative conflicts and negotiations.

The global level

At the global level, "policy" has to be established by multi-country agreements. Over the years, hundreds of international environmental agreements have been negotiated and implemented. Bilateral treaties are relatively uncomplicated two-country agreements. Many of these deal with managing international rivers (e.g., the Colombia River Treaty between the US and Canada). Others have been multilateral (e.g., the Convention for the Protection of the Mediterranean Sea Against Pollution, together with its numerous protocols). Table 6.1 shows a partial list of international agreements currently in force covering environmental matters.

Getting a collection of sovereign nations together to agree on a common action is normally fraught with conflict and controversy. Countries vary on a

Table 6.1 Partial list of international environmental agreements

Treaty	Year in force	Number of signatories to date
International Convention on Civil Liability for Oil Pollution Damages	1975	64
Agreement Concerning the International Commission for the Protection of the Rhine Against Pollution	1963	6
Convention on International Trade in Endangered Species	1975	182
Convention on Early Notification of a Nuclear Accident	1986	97
Montreal Protocol on Substances that Deplete the Ozone Layer	1989	175
Basel Convention on the Control of Transboundary Movements of Hazardous Wastes and their Disposal	1992	142
The Paris Agreement (under the UNFCCC)	2016	195

For a more complete list, see Barry C. Field and Martha K. Field (2021) *Environmental Economics An Introduction*, 8th edition, McGraw-Hill; and Scott Barrett (2003) *Environmental and Statecraft: The Strategy of environmental Treaty Making*. Oxford University Press.

wide range of features: small and large, developed and developing, growing and declining, democratic and less so, directly impacted and mostly unaffected, etc. Negotiations are usually difficult and time-consuming, and at the international level there is a lack of regulatory institutions effectively to enforce and implement the negotiated actions. This has become apparent, again, in negotiations about steps to reduce global climate change, which we will discuss in Chapter 10.

An agreement that offers useful lessons is the Montreal Protocol on Substances that Deplete the Ozone Layer. It grew from scientific evidence that the stratospheric ozone layer, critical for regulating solar radiation reaching the earth's surface, was being depleted by a type of chemical used heavily in refrigerators, air conditioners, and elsewhere. These are chlorofluorocarbons (CFCs), and the Montreal Protocol put in place a time schedule to phase out the production and consumption of these chemicals. In 2016 the Parties to the Montreal Protocol negotiated the Kigali Amendment to reduce the production and consumption of hydrofluorocarbons (HFCs), a substance that had been developed by chemical companies as a substitute for those named in the original agreement. HFC has been found to be a very potent global greenhouse gas. An important feature of the Montreal Protocol is that it gave developing countries a longer time interval to come into compliance, as compared to developed countries. It also contained a provision by which developed countries would create a large fund for compensating developing countries for the incremental costs of controlling emissions of the controlled substances. Montreal has been successful because it involved chemical companies and their competitive struggles to develop substitutes for the controlled substances.

Further reading

Barrett, S. (2003), *Environment and Statecraft: The Strategy of Environmental Treaty Making*, Oxford University Press, Oxford.

Coase, R.H. (1960), "Problem of Social Cost," *Journal of Law and Economics*, Volume 3, pp. 1–44.

Ostrom, E. (1990), *Governing the Commons: The Evolution of Institutions for Collective Action*, Cambridge University Press, Cambridge.

Serret, U. and N. Johnstone (2006), *The Distributional Effects of Environmental Policy*, Edward Elgar, Cheltenham UK and Northampton, MA, USA.

7 Pollution-control standards

ESSENTIAL SUMMARY

The control of environmental pollution to date has relied most heavily on the promulgation and enforcement of standards. A standard is a specification of behavior, or outcome, issued by public authorities and enforced through legal procedures. A pollution-control standard is one that addresses some aspects of the production and management of environmental pollutants. A limit on the quantity of emissions from a specific source is an example. Standards are often described as "command-and-control" because they rely on public authorities to issue and enforce specific rules and regulations governing the actions of polluters. Standards are attractive because they appear to mandate certain pollution-control activity, and because they conform to the polluter-pays principle, that it is polluters who should bear the cost of controlling environmental externalities. But economists criticize the reliance on standards because they are often not cost-effective. In this chapter, we discuss the economics of pollution-control standards.

Types of standards

A standard is a specification of behavior: authorities decide what behaviors will be acceptable, then mandate those behaviors in law, to be enforced by special means or through the normal legal machinery of the states. Informally it is called "command-and-control" because it directly specifies and enforces certain actions to be undertaken by polluters and regulators.

Pollution-control standards are popular because they appear to be direct and specific, setting specific limits on some aspect of the pollution-control process. They answer to the desire to bring about definite and timely changes in the behavior of polluters. It takes discretion away from polluters,

DOI: 10.4324/9781003143635-7

which for many people was the chief cause of pollution in the first place. Consider again the basic graph, presented in Chapter 3, showing abatement costs and environmental damages as they vary with the level of emissions. It would seem a simple job for authorities to put in place a regulation setting e* as the legal maximum of emissions, then send out the required inspectors and regulators to enforce it. In this sense, it would be like setting a highway speed limit. However, we know that setting and enforcing speed limits is much more complicated than it may seem, and the same is true for pollution-control standards.

"Standards" is also a term widely used in voluntary programs, as in, for example, the European Ecolabel system begun in 1992 whereby a product is deemed environmentally friendly and able to gain a European label attesting to that fact. Another example is the specifications many countries have adopted for environmental audits, such as compliance, risk, and health and safety audits. In this chapter, we will concentrate on regulatory standards.

We begin with a brief description of the types of standards used in pollution control:

- Emissions standards: maximum allowable emissions are usually expressed in terms of some physical quantity of emissions or maximum rate (quantity per minute or hour) over some time period. These are normally set for individual sources. Considering standards in the context of the basic model presented in Chapter 3, regulators would set maximum emissions per unit of time, such as tonnes of SO_2 per year. Other types of standards can be used, such as emissions per unit of an important input or emissions per unit of output. The nature of the production–emissions process involved dictates the specific standards that might be set. A type of emission standard that is used in some countries is a collective emission limitation. Examples are the "Total Pollutant Lead Regulation" of Japan and the "Total Maximum Daily Load" programs in the US. In considering an environmental feature such as a lake or wetland, regulators estimate the maximum total load of pollutants that may be allowed to keep its ambient levels below some benchmark. This load is then divided among sources on the lake or wetland.
- Ambient standards: these are maximum allowable quantities of pollutants in the ambient environment, often expressed in parts per million or per cubic meters of area. An example is a maximum allowable E. coli content of water in order to be deemed safe for swimming.
- Technology standards: these are requirements that polluters use a particular type of technology in their operation. A requirement that coal-fired power plants use stack-gas scrubbers is a technology standard.

- Performance standards: this is a generic name for any standard that requires some level or type of performance by polluter or potential polluter. A requirement that managers of a water treatment facility withhold certain emissions during periods of low flow; a requirement that airport operations (landings and takeoffs) be stopped at night; a requirement that farmers reduce their use of a particular pesticide below some level, are performance standards. An emission standard can be thought of as a type of performance standard.

Emission standards

Emission standards are essentially never-exceed levels on the direct outflow of environmental pollutants from their source. The most prominent example of emission standards is the system of tailpipe standards for cars and trucks established in the EU, the US, and in other countries. Emission standards are also widely used to control stationary industrial emissions.

Setting the standard

The most controversial issue of any standard is simply at what level it is set. In the real world of environmental regulation some people will want it set high, or more tightly, and some people will want the opposite. From an economic standpoint, standards should be set with some reference to their benefits in terms of reduced environmental damages, and to their cost in terms of what society gives up when setting a standard at some level. This argues for using a benefit-cost framework to determine the level of any standard.

Setting a standard implies taking some position with respect to the two main factors involved: the damages stemming from the emissions and the costs of abating them. Controversies arise over the extent to which regulators are allowed or encouraged to take a "balancing" approach, that is, whether they may legally take into account both abatement costs and reduced damages, or whether they must privilege one side or the other. In some cases, allowable emissions may be set at zero on the basis of high damage costs; this is what occurred when the insecticide DDT was outlawed in the US in 1972. In other cases, emission standards may be set at low levels on the assumption that very low levels have negligible effects. There is often controversy about whether such emission "thresholds" exist, and whether they might be different for different groups of people. Standards for radiation, for example, have been controversial in this respect. Standards for chemical exposure have also encountered this issue.

A balancing approach to emissions standards implies that regulators will consider the costs to polluters of lowering their emissions. The issue here is how regulators can get accurate information about these costs. The situation is one of "asymmetric information." The polluters themselves will usually have a better understanding than the standard setters regarding the cost of meeting standards of various degrees of stringency. The continuing problem is how the regulator can elicit accurate information about these costs from members of the polluting community since the cost information is typically private. There may be a natural tendency for polluters to exaggerate when queried about the expected costs of proposed emission reduction goals.

This clearly shows the importance of having accurate data about pollution damages, linking emissions with exposure and health outcomes. This is the normal work of epidemiologists and health scientists; good policy requires that they be strongly represented.

Cost-effectiveness

Emissions standards are normally faulted on grounds of cost-effectiveness, of getting emission reductions but at a much higher cost than necessary. The problem arises from a tendency for pollution-control programs to apply the same standards for all participating firms. If the firms differ a lot in their abatement costs (some old firms, some new; some using one production technology, others using a different one), pollution control would be more cost-effective overall if these differences were taken into account in controlling overall emissions. In particular, if sources with lower abatement costs achieve greater emission cutbacks, and those with higher abatement costs have lesser reductions. This problem was encountered early in the era of industrial air pollution control. Firms with multiple plants (multiple sources) were faced with applying the same emission standard at each plant. What evolved was a "bubble" policy, which treated these plants as a single source. The firm could then rebalance production, and thus pollution control, among the plants. The rule for cost-effectiveness when multiple sources contribute to the same pollution problem is that they should be adjusted so that marginal abatement costs should be the same for each. This is not so much a problem if sources have similar abatement costs, but it does become one when abatement costs differ substantially among them. In that case, applying the same emission limits to all of them sacrifices cost-effectiveness for policy simplicity.

The same can be said for differences among sources on the damage side. If the emissions of a group of sources are uniformly mixed it would argue for a common emission standard. But when the individual sources differ in terms of the damages they produce, uniform emission standards again achieve administrative simplicity at the cost of overall cost-effectiveness.

There is a wider problem as regards standards and incentives: setting a standard at one point in a pollution process may have an effect on other essential parts of the process. If an automobile standard is set, for example, on maximum emissions of CO_2 per mile, this will have no effect on another prime way of reducing air pollution from cars: by driving fewer overall miles.

An aspect of emission standards is that under normal circumstances there would appear to be no, or very weak, incentives to go beyond the standard, that is, to reduce emissions more than the standard, even though the cost of doing so might be modest.

Emission standard setting, in fact any type of standard setting, is subject to the possibility of "perverse incentives." These are incentives that tend to pull polluters away from more effective pollution control rather than toward it. Standards are often set in reference to the abatement costs of currently available technology. The assumption is that if pollution-control costs were to decrease, regulators would tighten the appropriate emissions. Then, to avoid this tightening, polluting firms may have a weaker incentive to adopt lower-cost pollution-control technology. A well-known example of this exists among older fossil power plants in the US: when older plants are upgraded with new technology for controlling airborne emissions, they are subject to tighter emission standards. This weakens the incentive that operators of these older plants have to upgrade their production and pollution-control technology. A classic case of perverse incentives is mileage standards for cars, in the name of using less fuel in the transportation sector. But this means cars are actually less costly per mile to drive, which will lead drivers to increase their total miles driven.

Ambient standards

An ambient standard is a maximum allowable pollutant level within a designated portion of the ambient or surrounding environment. It is often expressed in terms of concentration over some time period, e.g., a maximum of 0.5 parts per million of sulfur dioxide averaged over a three-hour period. It could be a limit, e.g., no discernable amount of asbestos. It could be based on an activity, e.g., water that is swimmable and fishable. The key is that it refers to a level of environmental quality to be attained, or maintained, in some part of the environment. They are immediately relevant because they refer to parts of the environment that directly affect humans, e.g., the air we breathe or the water we drink. Ambient standards can be put into place both as realistic goals and as aspirational goals to motivate further efforts in pollution control.

The obvious thing about ambient standards is that the environment itself connects ambient conditions back to actual emissions, as Figure 7.1 depicts.

The workings of the environment –wind patterns, water flows, temperature, etc., as well as emissions themselves, determine ambient pollution levels.

Setting ambient standards requires establishing the geographical areas to be included. There is a trade-off between defining a fine-grained set of regions, which require monitoring and sampling, and broad areas that require fewer resources to administer. To some extent the definition of ambient areas will be determined by the functioning of the relevant ecosystems. Another important factor is the geographical layout of political and administrative districts, and whether ambient environmental regions should be defined with these in mind. Actions to manage pollution and maintain ambient quality levels may be easier if the ambient regions conform to administrative regions. In the US, prime administrative management of ambient environments is assigned to the individual states. In the EU, the initiative resides with each member country in the context of an overarching EU Air Quality Directive. With Brexit, the UK is no longer under the EU Directive.

Figure 7.1 illustrates that if ambient conditions are to be managed, limits have to be placed on the various sources that contribute to these conditions.

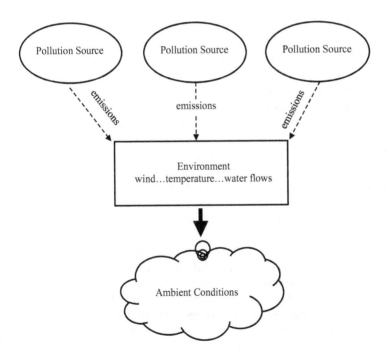

Figure 7.1 Ambient conditions from multiple sources

If only one source is responsible, say a single large industrial plant, it's unambiguous who would be controlled. But if there are multiple sources, and their emissions are uniformly mixed, some procedure or rule must be set on how the required reductions in total emissions are to be divided among them. This is a problem where the economic and political will likely conflict. As mentioned above, cost-effectiveness requires sources to be regulated according to their individual abatement costs; from a political standpoint, the pressure may be to apply the same standards to all sources. This is a huge problem in cases where economies are growing, while ambient conditions are already at maximum pollution limits. One common response is to hold new sources to tighter standards than established sources. Another, which was pioneered in California in the early days of air quality control, is to require that new sources buy emission rights from existing sources. Another common problem is where the failure to attain ambient standards in one region is because of emissions from sources in another region.

Technology standards

A technology standard is a requirement that polluters adopt and operate a specific type of technological means to control emissions. A requirement that power plants install stack-gas scrubbers to remove sulfur from stack gases is a technology standard. Another is a requirement that cars with internal combustion engines have certain devices for stopping the emissions of volatile organic compounds. Technology standards are especially common for reducing safety risks associated with industrial activity.

Technology standards are widely used in environmental regulation. In the early years of modern pollution-control, monitoring technology was underdeveloped, so monitoring and enforcement could focus on inspection to determine if sources were using approved technologies. This is still a major consideration in situations where emissions are hard to monitor, such as those involving chemical use. There was also a great deal of uncertainty about the actual costs of abating emissions in various industries, so setting technology requirements was an effort to ensure that abatement costs would be economically feasible.

Emission standards and technology requirements are often used in conjunction with one another. For particular industries, regulators determine how different technological options produce different levels of emissions, then set emission standards that relate to a specific technology. Sources then can be emissions compliant by using the approved production and pollution-control technology. In this way an emission standard essentially functions as a technology requirement. In the US, this is called "technology-based effluent standards" (TBES). For this to work, some criteria have to be used to identify acceptable technologies upon which to base emission standards. In effect, a balance must be reached of what a particular technology would cost and what it would accomplish in terms of emission reduction. The concept of a "Best Available Technology" has been adopted by many countries, as well as by the European Union. In circumstances where work procedures are at issue, not simply technical means, reliance is often put on "best management practices" (BMP). The regulation of agriculture is frequently based on BMPs because much of the pollution is non-point source and not easily measurable.

On the one hand the technology standards have definite strengths. They require that polluters take specific, verifiable steps that will reduce pollution. Criteria can be fine-tuned to give a range of technical options: e.g., "best available technology" versus "best practicable technology" versus "best economically viable technology." They can be verified without sophisticated and expensive emissions monitoring. They can be set at the level of an individual plant, or for an industry. But the strength of technology standards may also be a weakness, because they may diminish the incentive polluters have to find and adopt new and better technologies. In effect, they take the problem of finding the best pollution-control technology out of the hands of the polluters and put it in the hands of the regulators. In some cases, the regulators may know more about the technology option than the polluters. This was so in the US when catalytic converters became available to reduce pollution from automobiles. But it is often not the case; technology mandates can effectively lock in an inferior technology from the standpoint of pollution control.

The other problematic aspects of technology mandates are their tendency to be applied uniformly to all polluters. As we have seen several times above, the most cost-effective approach to reducing emissions among a collection of sources is to take advantage of the differences among them, if they exist, in their pollution-control costs. Technological standards, by treating all sources alike, basically violate this principle. The same is true for emission standards, which also tend to be applied uniformly across sources.

One useful aspect of technology standards is that they may lend themselves to "technology transfer." This is the process whereby technical and economic information about pollution control undertaken by "first adopters," becomes more readily available to later adopters.

Environmental standards and compliance

Nothing is more common than environmental standards that are announced with enthusiasm but not followed with equally enthusiastic steps to assure high rates of compliance. It is common in the developing world where enforcement institutions are weak and the emphasis is on economic growth. But it is an issue everywhere. Increasing the rates of compliance is costly. It is costly for individual sources, and it is costly for regulatory agencies that seek higher compliance or rates in general throughout an industry or region.

The economics of compliance divides the process into essentially two steps: (1) monitoring, to identify violators and violations; and (2) enforcement, to motivate and move violators to a higher state of compliance.

Compliance monitoring

Monitoring provides the basic data needed to evaluate compliance. Data on stationary, point-sources may be the most straightforward. Most countries have protocols and procedures for the public acquisition of environmental data. Differences normally exist between sources that can have a major impact on ambient conditions, local, regional, or national; and those that do not. There is usually a difference between large sources, which can install and operate advanced technology such as continuous emissions monitoring, and smaller sources, which cannot. In many situations and countries, heavy reliance is put on self-monitoring and reporting.

Since abatement is costly and regulation driven, and since regulatory actions are probabilistic to some extent, we would normally expect some degree of non-compliance under the theory that regulated firms would trade-off the costs of complete compliance with the risks of having to deal with a penalty of some type. This may be generally true, but research has also shown that in some cases a substantial amount of over-compliance may happen. Why would firms ever over-comply? One possibility is that with environmental issues more widely in public discussion, firms may find a competitive advantage in having a greener reputation in situations where information on compliance is publicly available.

Monitoring non-point source emissions is obviously different. Reliance here is normally placed on ensuring that best management practices, or certain technologies, are in place and being operated. These are technical and managerial routines that are known to result in reduced emissions, even though they may not be measured exactly.

Cars, trucks, and other mobile sources, since they are ubiquitous, are a special case. Nearly all countries have established emissions standards for vehicles in the form of allowable emissions per kilometer. Over time, these standards have been lowered, meaning that the fleet of cars currently on the road is a mix of vehicles with different emissions performance. Since the only effective way of lowering emissions, especially of CO_2, is to produce vehicles that get better fuel mileage, there is a rebound effect. In the US, emission tests are performed on in-use cars. There are no fines for cars that fail the test, just a requirement to repair in order to drive. In the EU, tests are performed on new cars.

Monitoring and enforcing ambient standards is much more complicated because it requires extrapolating from the condition of the environment to specific sources that are thought to be responsible. Different countries have different numbers of regions for monitoring ambient conditions (e.g., Bulgaria has three; Italy has almost 20). One important problem is that ambient conditions in one location or region may be heavily affected by emissions from sources in another location. This can arise from the flow patterns of wind and water. This recalls the celebrated case in the US where power plants in the Midwest, in order to reduce local air pollution, built taller smokestacks to carry their emissions off to the east. The same phenomenon of interregional air flows is important in Europe, carrying airborne emissions from west to east. Water pollution control can encounter the same problem, especially in river flow patterns. To enforce ambient standards and attain ambient conditions, some mechanism has to be put in place to go from the standards to specific emission limitations. In the US, this is the purview of "State Implementation Plans," and in Europe these are "National Air Pollution Control Programs." These programs depend heavily on studies to clarify the relationships between specific emission sources and ambient conditions.

Monitoring technology standards begins with the job of observing that the designated technology is installed. This is "initial compliance." To determine "continued compliance" it has to be ascertained whether the technology is, and has been, operating as specified. To do this a set of customary and legal conditions have to be worked out for when and how inspectors may have the necessary access to pollution sources and the technology.

Monitoring accidental release is another matter. Accidents are, by nature, episodic, so enforcement is tied up with preparation for, and reaction to, situations involving risk. The risk profiles differ markedly for different situations. Coastal oil spills of small or medium size are so frequent in most parts of the world that there is almost a continuous occurrence of spills over time, like fuel leakage with the transition of crude oil from a tanker to a land-based storage tank. At the other end are the massive spills that are infrequent but make the headlines, like the Deep-Water Horizon explosion in the Gulf of Mexico or the MT Haven disaster off the coast of Italy.

Compliance sanctioning

Sanctioning means taking appropriate actions to obtain adequate levels of compliance. It is often called "compliance assurance" because it includes more than just street penalties. It has a strong association with variations in cultural norms. For example, in Japan authorities place great reliance on invoking social attitudes about consensus, while in the US there is a heavy reliance on monetary fines and penalties. In France, there is a formal procedure for dealing with sources that are non-compliant, but many are dealt with on an informal basis. In India, enforcement has been largely ad hoc, and is hampered by the widespread thought that enforcement is a major impediment to economic growth. Levying fines for violations, or accidents, is normally done with the expectation that the larger the penalty the greater the likelihood that polluters will take steps to lower the probabilities of future violations. Research in the US shows that this relationship holds in reality. Whether fines should be higher or lower is a recurring conflict for policy makers.

"Softer" sanctioning refers to the efforts agencies make to help sources come into greater compliance through consulting, counseling, and convincing them to move in that direction. Enforcement is done both to get higher compliance by target sources and to create a climate of deterrence that will increase the general compliance rate in the future.

The idea of compliance assurance raises the economic question of what the optimal amount of compliance might be. From society's standpoint, compliance costs are social costs that must be added to private compliance costs to find the total costs of emissions reduction. From the standpoint of individual firms there is a trade-off between the reduction in abatement costs from non-compliance and the added risk of a fine or penalty levied by regulators.

Further reading

Faure, M.G. and R.A. Partain (2019), *Environmental Law and Economics, Theory and Practice*, Cambridge University Press, Cambridge.

Palmer, K., et al. (1995), "Tightening Environmental Standards the Benefit-Cost or the No-Cost Paradigm," *Journal of Economic Perspectives*, Volume 9, Number 4, pp. 119–132.

Shimsback, J.P. (2014), "The Economics of Environmental Monitoring and Enforcement," *Annual Review of Resource Economics*, Volume 6, pp. 339–360.

8   Pollution charges

ESSENTIAL SUMMARY

The economics of pollution control focuses on environmental externalities, the spillovers from private decisions made by producers and consumers. Externalities are real social costs, but they are unpriced. Therefore, they are not included in the normal market prices of goods and services. This strongly suggests that a way to correct this situation is for regulators to levy monetary charges to cover the environmental costs. Then the subsequent price of the good or service will include both the private costs and the environmental costs of their production and consumption. Pollution charges are a type of incentive-based regulation because they do not dictate the particular means that polluters must follow to reduce pollution. Faced with a price for the environmental consequences of their actions, they would have the incentive to reduce their environmental footprints with the most cost-effective means.

Emissions charges: the theory

There are many environmentally related charges in place around the world; mostly these are regarded as taxes because they are levied by governments, local or national. There are vehicle taxes, fuel taxes, landfill taxes, chemical taxes, waste treatment taxes, and so on. Most of these taxes are for the purpose of raising revenues, an objective all governments have to some extent. In this chapter, we will focus on the economics of emission taxes. An emission tax is a particular type of tax. In economics it is called a Pigouvian tax, after the economist A.C. Pigou who, in 1920, wrote a book suggesting that taxes could be used to correct the failure of private markets to include the value of environmental externalities. So a Pigouvian tax, or charge, is

DOI: 10.4324/9781003143635-8

a levy put into effect specifically to rectify an externality. Of course a tax will raise revenues, but that is not its main purpose: its main objective is to correct an externality.

In this chapter, we deal with emission charges, a term that we will use synonymously with emissions taxes. How an emission charge works at the level of the firm is depicted in Figure 8.1. It shows the marginal abatement cost of a single source. The horizontal axis is labeled in terms of the quantity of emissions, increasing to the right. The vertical axis is labeled in monetary units. The curve labeled MAC shows the firm's marginal abatement costs. At any point on the curve it shows the added cost of reducing emissions by another unit. Alternatively, it shows the amount by which costs would decrease if emissions were to be a unit higher. The marginal abatement cost rises to the left, that is, as emissions are reduced. This represents an assumption that mirrors reality: as emissions are reduced the added abatement cost of further reduction increases.

We can assume that an unregulated firm would put little or no expense into emission reduction; therefore, its emissions would be at e_0. An emission charge is now introduced, at a level indicated by C on the vertical axis. This is a charge of C dollars, or euros, or whatever currency, per unit of emissions. Since the charge is constant at all levels of emissions, it is shown as a horizontal line. Now a firm could reduce its total costs of production by reducing emissions. Starting at e_0, it pays in abatement costs an amount less than it would pay in the emission charge. As it reduces emissions its abatement cost for continued reduction increases, until at e_1 these two costs,

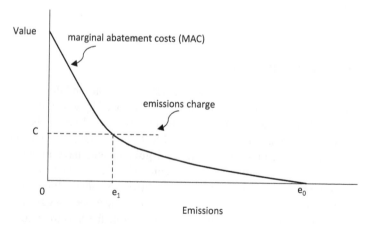

Figure 8.1 Emission charge

the costs of abatement and the costs of emission tax, are equal. That is this firm's best response under the emission charge. If the charge were increased, it would choose a lower emission rate. And vice versa.

Would the firm just maintain its original emission rate, pay the charge, and pass the cost off to consumers? We assume that the firm has the objective of maximizing its net income and faces active competition within its industry. It therefore wants to keep its costs down and cannot afford to charge prices above its competition. Under these circumstances the firm would search for ways of using less of the factor that has gone up in price, namely its emissions of pollutants. This is why it is called an incentive-based approach to pollution reduction. The firm has an incentive, and a means, of looking around for the least costly way of reducing emissions. The important point is that it is not necessary for regulators to know what the best abatement technology is for the sources. The sources themselves are being relied upon to find the least costly way of reducing their emissions. This addresses the "asymmetric information" problem, in which polluting firms normally have a better understanding of how to cost-effectively reduce emissions than do the regulating authorities. The emission charge gives polluters the incentive to use this private information to reduce environmental pollution.

Sources here are essentially balancing two costs: the costs of abating emissions, and the costs of an emissions tax. Abatement costs are real social costs in the sense that they involve the expenditure of productive inputs to produce something, namely, a reduction in emissions. The emission tax payments, however, are what are called transfer payments. These are payments made by the firm (and ultimately the customers of these firms) for the right to make the emissions.

Another factor that needs to be attended to is multi-media substitutions. In some cases it may be technically feasible to reduce one type of emission, e.g., a wastewater emission, by switching to another type of emission, for example an airborne emission. Regulators clearly have to be aware of these options. One approach is for a tax on a certain type of residual to be levied irrespective of which part of the environment it is discharged into.

We note that after the firm adjusts to the charge, it will be operating at an emission level where its marginal abatement costs are equal to the charge. This leads us to a conclusion about industry cost-effectiveness. When there are multiple polluters, overall cost-effectiveness requires that once they have made their adjustments in their emissions, they all will be operating at exactly the same marginal abatement cost. If they were not, it would be possible for regulators to get more overall emission reduction at the same overall cost by shifting emissions away from the higher cost sources and toward the lower cost ones. An emission charge meets this cost-effectiveness criterion, because if the same charge is applied throughout the industry, all the firms in the industry will end up with the same marginal abatement costs.

Setting the charge

At what level should the charge be set? For this we return to the idea expressed in Chapter 3 about the socially efficient level of emissions. That level is the one that equates, on the margin, the social costs of pollution damages with the marginal abatement costs for the economy in question. The economic rule to follow, then, is that for social efficiency the emission charge should be set at the level of marginal pollution damages. If we are dealing here with a uniformly mixed pollutant stemming from a group of sources, then the marginal damages are the same for all the sources. This is the case, for example, of carbon dioxide emissions stemming from fossil fuels. For other pollutants, the damages from different sources may vary because of their locations, or because of wind or water flows that affect their emissions. Cost-effectiveness in this case requires different charges for the sources. Naturally, this puts a burden on regulators because it relies on separate damage relationships being determined for each source. More feasible is the idea of establishing a uniform charge for all similar sources in a defined region. In places where charges have been used regulators have mostly opted for the administrative simplicity of uniform charges.

Incidence: who actually pays

It is the polluting firms that pay the charge, at least nominally. This is a positive feature of the approach: it conforms to the ethical notion called the "polluter pays principle," that is, it should be the polluters themselves who bear the cost of reducing pollution. But private firms are involved with producing goods and services for consumers, so when pollution charges become part of their production costs, they will be passed on to consumers in some degree. This is not inconsistent with the comment above about firms paying the tax and continuing to pollute. When the tax is levied, sources will adjust their inputs in order to minimize total costs. These total costs of course will have increased because what they were getting free before the tax, now has a price on it. It is these total costs which will be passed on to their customers.

If an industry is composed of a number of similar firms, in competition with one another, and an emission charge is levied on all, we would expect the emission tax to be completely passed on to consumers. By how much will depend on the technologies available to abate emissions. If the aggregate output of this industry decreases because of diminished demand for its output, a portion of the burden of the pollution tax will be felt through diminished employment in the industry.

If an emission charge is levied on one firm, or a small group of firms, within a competitive industry, the regulated firms may find it impossible to pass on these costs through output price increases. If demand shifts to unregulated firms, the owners and workers in the regulated firms will bear the costs. This is a major reason that firms often cite for opposing emission charges: that it diminishes their competitive position with their rivals. It is an important factor, for example, when regulators in one community, or one region, adopt pollution-control measures that create a competitive burden for firms in the region. This is especially relevant in the campaign to reduce greenhouse gas emissions.

If an emission charge is levied on a monopolist (e.g., an electricity utility), we would expect the price of their output to increase, but by how much is a question. Monopolists (single firms within an industry) and oligopolists (a few firms) have some degree of control over their prices. So the burden of the pollution charge will be divided in some fashion between consumers, workers, and owners, and it is impossible to predict without detailed knowledge of the industry. With globalization this can have important implications for what is called "leakage," which means the deflection of production away from firms subject to emission limitations toward firms that are not, possibly those in another country. The possibility of leakage adds to the need for coordinated action by multiple governments, in this case to have a unified emission charge across jurisdictions. We will encounter this problem again when we discuss the economics of a carbon tax in Chapter 10. Public utilities (suppliers of electricity, water, internet service, and others) are normally regulated monopolists. So how the ultimate division of the charge is distributed to consumers, owners, and workers is the result of negotiations between public utility commissions and the firms.

Firms subject to an emission charge have sometimes argued that it is unfair for them to have to bear the cost of reducing emissions, in addition to the charge on remaining emissions. And it is true that under some circumstances individual firms could be paying more in total emission charges than the total damages they are causing. If regulators are sympathetic to this argument, they could put in place a two-part charge; with a low or zero charge for emissions up to a certain threshold level, and a full charge at higher levels.

If the emission charge leads to substantial price increases, questions come up about how it impacts consumers with low or moderate incomes. This is one reason why emission charges that have been tried in various countries have been mostly kept to modest levels. A running objection to environmental taxes like an emission tax is the idea that any product price increases they cause will impact disproportionately on lower income consumers. These emission taxes could improve the environment but make worse another social issue, such as income inequality or disparity. How much worse depends on several things. One is the impact of price increases on various types of goods. Price increases on necessities, such as food and public transportation, will affect low-income households more than taxes on luxuries. There are ways of offsetting the impacts of these price charges, particularly using the tax proceeds stemming from the emissions charge. There is difficulty in targeting income relief specifically to those who have been hurt by the price increases. We will discuss this in greater detail below.

Emission charges and uncertainty

The goal of emission charges is to produce a reduction in emissions and the damage they cause. Sources will adjust to a charge according to their own abatement costs. But what if the regulators don't know exactly what the marginal abatement cost functions are? This is a very normal situation; actual pollution-control costs are private information. But in this case the regulators will be uncertain about how much emissions will be reduced with taxes of different amounts. If the charge is too low, emissions will be too high and there will be pressure to increase the tax, and vice versa if the charge is too high. Consider again Figure 8.1. It is the shape of marginal abatement cost function that will determine a firm's response to a charge on emissions. Suppose the actual, but unknown to regulators, abatement function is very shallow in its slope. Then an emission charge will have big leverage on emissions. A small increase in the charge will lead to a relatively large decrease in emissions, and vice versa. Conversely, if the unknown abatement cost function is steep the opposite occurs – large changes in the charge will have a relatively small effect on emissions. This obviously creates a conundrum. Regulators are left knowing the tax, but not knowing the quantity of emissions that will result when it is put in place. The conundrum is sharpened when regulators consider that technical change will shift the abatement cost relationship over time, and therefore shift emissions. The uncertain effect on emissions is one reason that emission charges have not become more popular.

Charges on output

Often it is difficult to measure emissions, but less difficult to measure the quantity of output from the polluting firms. This suggests that charges could be set on output, on the assumption that this will feed back and reduce the pollution coming from production. The issue here is how close the connection is between the quantity of output and the quantity of emissions stemming from that output. To illustrate, consider the following expression. It is a way of breaking down total emissions into the constituent steps that make it up. It refers to emissions of CO_2 from cars.

$$\text{Total Emissions} = \text{Number of people} \times \text{Cars per person}$$
$$\times \text{Mileage per car} \times \text{Emissions per mile}$$

A tax on automobiles in general will act to reduce the number of autos per person (the third term in the expression) but would do nothing to motivate users to take actions that would reduce emissions of the car, for example by driving less and driving more slowly. If the tax was set higher on less fuel-efficient cars, then there would be fewer of those bought, and therefore less total emissions. This is the rationale for taxing less efficient cars, or appliances, more highly. In addition, if there was a tax on an essential input in these items, such as fuel in cars, this would impact the last term in the expression, emissions per unit of the item. Fuel taxes are common around the world, though there are some countries where fuel subsidies are still in place.

Emission charges and revenue recycling

Emission charges lead a double life, however. They have an effect on emissions, and they lead to increased public revenues. For many people the revenues are more of an attraction than the possible impacts on emissions. The revenue aspect of taxes shifts the perspective somewhat, from reducing emissions to accumulating tax revenues. In theory, the revenue flow will depend on the elasticity, in effect the slope, of the abatement cost function. The steeper it is the more revenues will increase as the tax is increased.

The distributional effects of environmental taxes can be offset to a greater or lesser extent by recycling the tax revenue. Graduated income payments, or subsidies of goods or services disproportionately used by low-income families, such as public transportation, would substantially lower the distributional impacts of the taxes. Suggestions have been made for using the environmental tax revenue to lower other taxes, such as, in the US, the payroll tax used to fund the social security system.

What else might be done with the revenues? One possibility is to subsidize other useful behavior. In a deposit-refund system there is a tax applied to the purchasers of something, for example a bottle of sugary drink or soda, then the revenues from the tax are used to subsidize the safe return and disposal or recycling of the empty bottle. Another possibility is to use the tax revenues to compensate for lowering another tax. In the United States, for example, there is a tax on worker payrolls that is earmarked for the support of social security. The emission tax revenue could be used to offset the lowering of the payroll tax. So the tax on the bad is used to offset the reduction of a tax on something that is good (employment). Another potential use of emission tax revenue is to offset the effects of price effects on consumers. Tax revenue could be parceled out to certain consumers, for whom the price effects of the emission taxes have been large or inequitable.

Emission taxes are common in some European countries. Taxes on SO_2 and NO_x emissions have been instituted in Sweden, France, Italy, Switzerland, and Spain. These taxes are often used as complements to command-and-control regulations with standards. In Sweden, the resources from the NO_x and SO_2 taxes are fully refundable to the firms in the industries that paid the tax. In France, the tax revenues are used to subsidize pollution-related investments by the tax-paying firms. The recycling of the tax revenues has strengthened the acceptance of emissions taxes, which have had a significant impact on emissions.

Emission charges and innovation

The conclusion on pollution control standards, which are considered in the last chapter, is that they don't provide a strong incentive for polluters to innovate, to find new and more cost-effective ways of reducing emissions. They may actually stultify innovation if polluters believe that regulators will respond to innovation by tightening the standards. Emission charges do not have this effect, at least in theory. By innovating and finding less costly ways of lowering emissions, polluters can lower their costs by lowering their pollution tax payments. In this way the incentives of polluters are aligned with the desires of society in general, to find newer and better ways of pollution control. Another aspect of this is that, unlike standards, emission charges will lead polluters to lower their emissions as their abatement costs shift downward. The essence of this is that the incentive effect of emission charges will continue to work even as sources find more cost-effective ways of lowering emissions. The incentive effect continues because savings in emission tax payments are possible with continued innovation.

Subsidies

A subsidy is basically a negative tax. It would appear that an emission subsidy could have the same effect as a tax. Look at Figure 8.1 again. Suppose instead of a tax of so much per unit of emissions, authorities offered a subsidy of the same amount per unit of emissions reduced, starting at the point where abatement costs are zero (e_0). A firm would then find it profitable to reduce emissions as long as the subsidy was more than the cost of abatement (above

MAC curve) and would stop reducing emissions where these two were equal. This is the same result, at least in terms of emissions, as in an emission tax.

The problem with subsidies to control emissions is that, although individual firms may lower their emissions, the industry itself may expand under the influence of the subsidies. The subsidies have the effect of lowering the overall marginal costs of the firms in the affected industry. Figure 8.2 shows the probable result of this. It shows a demand curve (D) and a supply curve (S_1) for an industry. Under standard conditions, markets yield a price of P_1 and quantity of Q_1. Suppose an emission subsidy is introduced. The effect of this is to lower costs in the industry, and shift the supply curve to the right, to S_2. The effective supply curve is now S_2, and a market equilibrium tends now toward a quantity of Q_2 and an effective price of P_2. Compared to the situation without the subsidy, output has increased from Q_1 to Q_2, the market price has decreased from P_1 to P_0. The subsidy is the difference between P_0 and P_2.

The important conclusion is that the introduction of the subsidy leads to an increase in quantity and a lowering of the price in the market, though not by as much as the subsidy. The effect of the subsidy is a possible expansion of the industry, which subsequently can cause an increase in total industry emissions, even though the subsidy may have decreased the emissions of each individual firm. More significantly, the price drop stimulates an increase in consumption. Although the subsidy lowers emissions for individual firms, the expansion of the industry from the influence of the subsidy could actually lead to an increase in the emissions of the industry as a whole.

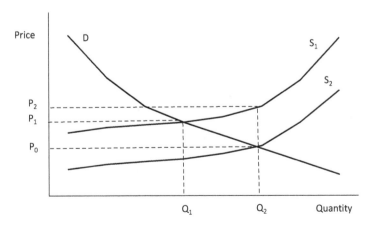

Figure 8.2 Effects of a subsidy

78   *Pollution charges*

Further reading

Pigou, A.C. (1920), *Economics of Welfare*, Macmillan, London.
Hoel, M. (1998), "Emission Taxes versus Other Environmental Policies," *Scandinavian Journal of Economics*, Volume 100, Number 1, pp. 79–104.
Miller, S. J. and M.A. Vela (2013), *Are Environmentally Related Taxes Effective?*, Inter-American Development Bank Working Paper Series, No IPD-WP-467.

9 Economics of emissions trading

ESSENTIAL SUMMARY

Emissions trading has become widespread in the campaign against pollution. One common type is a cap-and-trade (CAP) system, and another is offset trading. Cap-and-trade programs, like emission charges, are incentive-based plans. CAP programs work by authorities first setting the total quantity of emissions for a given set of sources. Permits are created corresponding to this total. These are distributed among participating sources and are tradable. Since the total supply of permits (sometimes called allowances) is fixed, trading creates a market price for permits, which becomes the price incentive for firms to control their emissions. The first significant CAP program was the US plan to control SO_2 emissions from power plants. The European Trading Scheme is a multi-country CAP program for controlling CO_2 emissions. Virtually any situation where individual emissions streams are measurable can be managed with a carefully designed CAP program. Economists are divided over whether CAP programs are more effective than emission charge plans to bring about cost-effective pollution control. Trading without a CAP, especially trading in carbon offsets, has become very popular in the effort to reduce global climate change.

Cap-and-trade: the principle

A cap-and-trade plan begins by identifying a group of sources that will fall within the program. It will be the emissions of these sources that will be controlled, which will limit them to point-source and measurable forms of emissions, or emissions that can be estimated with accuracy. Authorities then establish an overall limit or "cap" to the sum of all emissions from

DOI: 10.4324/9781003143635-9

sources in the plan. Most CAPs are multi-year, so the total annual emissions will be defined over a period of time. Usually the cap declines over time, so total overall emissions decrease. The authority defines emission permits, called allowances, equal in number to the total allowable emissions. Each permit corresponds to a unit (usually a tonne) of emissions. The permits are distributed to the participating sources. In many cases, they are distributed at no cost; sometimes they are auctioned. The initial permit award for each source consists of a sequence of dated permits extending over the life of the program. The permit holdings of each source put a limit on its emissions. A polluter holding 100 permits for the current year, for example, must hold its emissions at or below 100 for that year. The permits are tradeable. A source has a choice to make each year: to hold its permits for that year; to buy more permits for that year; or to sell some of its permits for that year. Assuming all sources comply, the total emissions from the group will be no greater than the sum of the individual permit holdings.

Trades can take place over time, for example the buying and selling of permits applicable to a future year. Most CAP programs allow permit banking, i.e., a permit not used for the current year may be held and used in a future year. The buying and selling of permits creates a price for them. It is the price that creates the incentive aspects of the plan. A firm will compare the going price with its abatement cost, and if the former exceeds the latter, the firm can improve its position by reducing its emissions and selling the permits it now no longer needs. Another firm sees that abatement costs exceed the going permit price and can improve its situation by abating less and buying permits to cover its higher emissions. Trading takes place under the cap; what changes is not the overall emissions level but how it is distributed among the sources.

CAP programs can be especially useful when abatement costs differ substantially among sources. Figure 9.1 shows a simple case of two polluting firms and depicts how trading emission permits can make both of them better off. The two firms are labeled A and B and the marginal abatement costs of each, MAC_A and MAC_B. Their uncontrolled emissions are a_0 and b_0. A CAP program is now started. Each firm is given permits that would nominally require proportionate emission cutbacks, to a_1 and b_1, respectively. But making those two emission cutbacks would leave them with different marginal abatement costs. A's marginal abatement costs rise less steeply than B's, as emissions are reduced. Both firms can now gain by trading permits. Suppose the going price of permits is indicated on the vertical axes. Firm A can sell permits to B and become better off because the price of permits exceeds the additional costs of abatement for that firm. Firm B can gain because it can buy permits at a price that is lower than what it will save in abatement costs. Gains from trade will continue until firm A has emissions

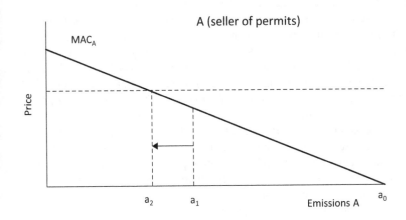

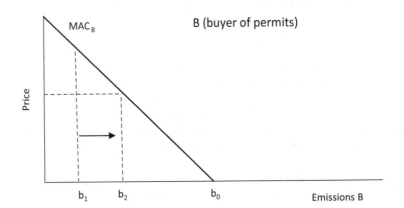

Figure 9.1 Emission trading example

of a_2 and firm B has emissions at b_2. Note that as permits are traded between the two firms the total emissions of the two firms remain constant. At the end of trading they will end up with marginal abatement costs the same, and equal to the price of permits.

A CAP plan begins with a public agency setting the overall emissions cap. The size of the cap is, of course, critical. Too many permits will result in prices that are too low, as in any supply–demand situation. If permit prices are too low they will have little influence in affecting firms' emission levels. This was a problem encountered in the early days of the European Trading Scheme (ETS), the first major multi-country cap-and-trade program. The surplus of permits initially drove their price to zero. The market of the ETS has since recovered. Of course, there can be the opposite problem; too few permits can lead to a price that is high and disruptive for an industry. One possible answer for this is for regulators to set a price ceiling (sometimes called a safety valve price), and then allocate additional permits whenever the ceiling is reached. The problem of prices being too low or too high is inherent in the CAP techniques because it is a quantity-setting plan and because regulators may not have accurate information about abatement costs.

Tradable emission permits are potentially valuable property rights, so how they are distributed among polluters is an important issue, on both efficiency and equity grounds. Very often permits are distributed initially by reference to past emission profiles. There may be a perverse incentive in this during the planning phase, if sources believe that higher current emissions will qualify them for higher permit allocations. From a theoretical perspective, the final distribution of emissions over sources is independent of the initial permit distribution. But the distribution of income from trading is not. Meaning that the initial distribution of permits can be based to some extent on political exigencies, for example, allocating more permits to sources whose political support is advantageous. Individual sources can be conflicted about wanting an ample supply of permits but realizing that if everybody gets an ample supply the resulting permit price will be low. As the experience with CAP programs has grown, regulators have turned more to auction markets to distribute permits. The advantage of auctions is that they become a source of revenues, analogous to the situation with emission taxes, which can be devoted to public programs or to reduce other taxes.

Cap-and-trade, like emission charges, is well suited for situations in which the different sources differ substantially in the costs of abating emissions. There can be a problem, however, if the emissions from the buying firm(s) produce greater damage, perhaps because of their location, than the emissions of the selling firm. If that happens a lot, it can lead to what is called the "hot-spot" problem, which is the accumulation of permits by a small number of sources that have a disproportionate impact on downwind or downstream damages. A way of avoiding this is for authorities to place limits on certain trades, either outright prohibitions, or by requiring some to be made on a disproportionate, rather than a one-to-one, basis.

Cap-and-trade programs have sometimes been criticized because sources which are buying permits may appear to be buying the "right to pollute." However, with the cap, if some sources are buying others must be selling. The total quantity of emissions remains constant. It is the trading part of the cap-and-trade that determines how the total emissions of the industry are distributed among the firms in the industry.

We saw in the chapter on emission charges that cost-effective pollution control was made possible because each source adjusted to the common emission charge. CAP programs attain cost-effectiveness through all the sources adjusting to the prevailing price for emission permits. Furthermore, the CAP approach (like emission charges) is an incentive-based approach; it allows individual sources to adopt what they themselves judge to be the most cost-effective way to reduce their emissions, as opposed to the traditional command-and-control approach based on various types of standards established and enforced by regulators.

Recall that each permit applies to emissions in a particular year. This opens additional opportunities for public regulators and for polluting firms. One possibility is to have a declining number of permits over time, either in total or for each firm. Another is that firms may swap permits applicable to this year's emissions for permits good for a future year. This allows firms to lease permits for a few years, perhaps to cover increased emissions during a plant changeover. The ability to trade in future permits provides a means of reducing the uncertainty associated with future permit prices.

The enforcement of a CAP plan is more complex than that of an emission charge. It requires that each source be monitored in terms of its emissions and its permit holdings. The problem of monitoring emissions is the same as with a charge system: accuracy, timeliness, and comprehensiveness. Regulators require a reasonably sophisticated system to monitor the flow of transactions and the holdings among polluters and all other participants: banks, brokers, outside groups, and so on. If a program is successful, the permits will have substantial value, which opens up the possibility of fraud and theft.

The administering agency also has the task of establishing and enforcing trading rules. A feature of CAP programs is that non-polluters have a way of participating and helping in determining the outcome of the program. They can do this by buying and retiring pollution permits, assuming that the rules permit market participation of non-polluters.

As in any pollution-control system there is a trade-off between cost and stringency of enforcement, and between stringency and the probability of future violations. Stringency in this case means how closely, and when, permit holdings have to cover emissions. In some CAP programs there is a reconciliation period, where sources are given time to acquire additional permits to cover any shortfall in permit holdings for the level of pollution being emitted.

CAP plans create markets, and markets can be volatile and uncertain. The aim of any CAP is to create a market price for the targeted emissions. The overall incentive effect of a CAP program is produced by the price of carbon being passed along through the "downstream" markets for goods and services according to their carbon content. The incentive effect of the price is weakened if it fluctuates unexpectedly. One thing that can cause this is to have changes in other related pollution-control programs. For example, many countries have renewable energy standards. Changes made to tighten these standards will have the effect of reducing the demand for CO_2 emission permits, driving permit prices down. Similar impacts can flow into the permit market from such programs as fuel economy standards, gasoline blending mandates, and solar subsidies. The problem is that volatile permit prices will not necessarily provide consistent, steady, and continuing incentives for vigorous pollution control, especially as these efforts will usually involve investment in long-lived pollution-control technology.

Cap-and-trade programs are being widely adopted for the control of global greenhouse gases (GHG). GHG are uniformly mixed and cumulative. They connect to the use of fossil fuels, which are used in almost all countries around the world. One of the first GHG CAPs was the Regional Greenhouse Gas Initiative (REGGI) formed by nine states in the northeastern part of the United States. California initiated a CAP for GHG in 2013. Similar programs have been started in New Zealand and parts of Australia, South Korea, Columbia, and others. We have already mentioned the European Trading Scheme, which is a multi-country CAP program for controlling greenhouse gas emissions. We will have more to say about CAPs and GHG in Chapter 10.

Trading without a CAP

It is possible to have a trading program without a CAP. One of the first instances of emission trading without a CAP was in California in the 1970s. The problem was how to allow economic growth without increases in total emissions in a region. The answer was to allow new firms to buy emission credits from existing firms.

Another type of trading is called "baseline and offset trading," which is slightly different from classic cap-and-trade. Each firm is given a certain quantity of emissions as a baseline. The source may then earn emission credits for any emissions below the baseline, which may be sold to firms who want emission permits to satisfy pollution-control requirements. Still another kind of trading is called "emission rate trading," or sometimes "basis and credit trading." A type of rate trading was used in the United States to reduce the overall social cost of shifting from leaded to unleaded fuel. Fuel refineries were given annual base rates for lead in fuel. Refineries that were able to convert to unleaded fuel quickly and at lower cost could sell lead credits to refineries that had higher conversion costs. This lowered the overall cost of making the change, without increasing the overall time for the industry to make the adjustment to lead-free gas.

Offset trading

Trading in carbon offsets has become a worldwide phenomenon. Offsets are theoretically created by anything that reduces the targeted emissions. For example, carbon offsets can be created by any activity that reduces carbon emissions, either actual emissions or expected emissions. Some examples are reforestation, renewable energy supply, and atmospheric carbon removal. A carbon offset is a reduction in greenhouse gases made to compensate for greenhouse gas emissions made elsewhere. Thus, for example, a firm wishing to compensate for its own GHG emissions might buy an offset, indicating that somewhere else GHG emissions have been reduced by a comparable amount. The first international offset program was the Clean Development Mechanism (CDM) of the Kyoto Protocol for reducing global greenhouse gases. This program allowed a country subject to an emission limit to implement emission reduction programs in countries of the developing world. A major objective of the CDM was to find a way to fund GHG reducing projects in countries that did not themselves have sufficient resources to support those efforts. The CDM process was essentially subsumed by the terms of the Paris Agreement. It is basically a formal market carried out by participating countries. The global carbon offset market is being linked to certain regulatory programs. Firms in the European Trading Scheme, for example, may satisfy a portion of their GHG reduction obligations by buying certified carbon offsets. Domestic offsets may be used if generated by projects in member states of the EU; international offsets may be used under strict limits. In the US, companies required to produce a certain number of zero emissions cars may purchase offsets generated by electric car producers. These offsets are often called "compliance offsets" because they are being used by sources to comply in part with regulatory requirements.

Voluntary offset markets have also become common. These offer a way for a person or group to purchase offsets to compensate, in whole or in part, for their carbon footprint. For example, an airline passenger may purchase offsets to compensate for the GHG produced during a flight. Or a person may purchase offsets to compensate for GHG emissions resulting from their operating a gas-guzzling car.

Offset markets first burgeoned in the 1990s and are expected to expand into the future as climate change policy develops. Part of the growth comes from their being integrated into regulatory cap-and-trade programs. Some come from the growing desire of individuals to participate directly in pollution control, especially that connected to global climate change. As part of the effort to combat global climate change, many firms and organizations have pledged to become carbon neutral. This will add to the future demand for offsets. But offsets and the offset market have been much criticized for what has come to be called "greenwashing," the creation and trading of fake or suspect offsets. These are offsets that have not been fully substantiated. This can happen because offsets may be created in remote or distant regions where their veracity cannot easily be verified.

Offsets can be problematic also because they may be based on counterfactuals, such as the promise not to cut down a forest when, realistically, that forest would not have been harvested anyway, offset or not. Further, an offset market can actually create a perverse incentive for conservation efforts. Any effort to decrease emissions outside the offset program works to decrease the potential supply of saleable offsets. This creates a disincentive if a region or country looks toward selling offsets as a way to generate revenue. There have been organized efforts to authenticate offsets that are supplied in offset markets. It has been important to adopt a set of criteria that are required for an offset to be legitimate. Some criteria are:

1. Reality: they must in fact be linked to an overt effort at reducing carbon emissions.
2. Additionality: the offsetting carbon-emitting activity must not be something that would have been done anyway (e.g., a reforesting program), but is done in response to the availability of offset demand.
3. Verifiable: the offset must be verified by somebody other than the individuals or groups whose actions have created that offset.
4. No double counting: it must be certified that the offset also has not been sold to another buyer.

It is no surprise that the offset market has become extensive and well organized, with public and private participants and intermediaries who facilitate the flow of offsets between sellers and buyers. Carbon offsets will play an increasing role around the world as countries, regions, industries, and firms all seek to lower their carbon footprint.

Further reading

Conte, M.N. and M.J. Kotchen (2010), "Explaining the Price of Carbon Offsets," *Climate Change Economics*, Volume 1, Number 2, pp. 93–111.

Dales, J.H. (1968), *Pollution, Property and Prices*, University of Toronto Press, Toronto.

Schmalensee, R. and R.N. Stavins (2017), "Lessons Learned from Three Decades of Experience with Cap and Trade," *Review of Environmental Economics and Policy*, Volume 11, Number 1, pp. 59–69.

Tietenberg, T. (2006), *Emissions Trading: Principles and Practices*, Routledge, London.

10   Global climate change

ESSENTIAL SUMMARY

Supreme among contemporary environmental pollution problems is the global phenomenon of climate change stemming from human actions. Carbon dioxide buildup in the earth's atmosphere will continue to lead to increased surface temperatures, higher ocean levels, and more violent storms. How rapidly these effects will happen is unclear. It is, therefore, uncertain how rapid the human response should be. Effective action requires individual country efforts to reduce emissions of greenhouse gases, and collective action at the global level. The Paris Agreement is the latest international effort to address global climate change. From an economic standpoint, the problem is that carbon is severely underpriced, which gives an incentive for its extensive use. One effective response is, therefore, to put a price on carbon, which can be done in several ways. Also, special efforts are needed to encourage technological innovation that shifts the energy system away from fossil fuels. Attention must also be devoted to studying efficient and equitable steps for adapting to a warming climate.

The problem

The pollution-control issue of supreme importance to the contemporary world is the influence of humans on the global climate, particularly from the use of fossil fuels. It is not something that has just been discovered. It was scientifically detailed over a century ago. For a long time it has been on the back burner of human concern; what has been on the front burner is economic growth and development to accommodate a burgeoning human population. No longer. We are now well aware that the airborne emissions

DOI: 10.4324/9781003143635-10

of an industrial economy, especially carbon dioxide, have a vast potential to change the global climate. It has been shown theoretically, and, with warmer temperatures and variable weather patterns, it has started to become apparent.

Climate change is the term used to describe these impacts of the atmospheric buildup of greenhouse gases. Emissions of greenhouse gases have inexorably followed the growth of industrial economies. The most prominent greenhouse gas, accounting for about 76 percent of the total, is carbon dioxide. Others are methane (16 percent) and nitrous oxide (6 percent). Carbon dioxide is a cumulative, persistent, and uniformly mixed pollutant on a global scale. In 1950, global emissions were estimated to have been about five billion tonnes; in 2020 they were about 38 billion tonnes. Carbon dioxide emissions are linked to fossil fuel combustion. About 36 percent come from electricity production, 38 percent from transportation, 15 percent from industrial heat requirements, and 11 percent from residential and commercial heating and cooling.

Since the middle of the twentieth century, CO_2 emissions have exceeded the earth's capacity to absorb them. The result has been a steady increase in the atmospheric CO_2 concentration. In 1950, this was about 280 parts per million (ppm). It is currently over 400 ppm and rising. The concentration of all greenhouse gases in 2020 is about 450 ppm.

It is important to understand the stock effect of GHG emissions, especially CO_2. Each year's emissions add to the accumulated global total, and it is the total that drives the earth's greenhouse effect and ultimately its temperature. Atmospheric CO_2 has a long residence time in the atmosphere: it is estimated, for example, that half of the CO_2 emitted in 1850 is still in the atmosphere. Some of the other greenhouse gases have shorter residence times: methane is 12 years, while NO_x is about a hundred years. The upshot of this is that, to have an impact, emission reduction will have to be larger and permanent.

The damage function

Atmospheric greenhouse gases (GHG) are linked to the earth's radiation balance. Scientific estimates are that each doubling of the concentration will increase the earth's surface temperature from 1.5 to 4.5°C. On this basis, estimates are that if GHG emissions continue to increase as they have in the past, the main surface temperature of the earth could rise by about 2°C by 2050, and by about 4.2°C by 2100. These temperature rises could be decreased if GHG emissions are reduced.

Scientists have studied the impacts of temperature increases on the earth's physical systems. These include:

- Sea-level rise
- Increase in storm frequency and intensity
- Droughts and heat waves
- Rapid change in Greenland and Antarctic ice sheets

These impacts will affect humans in many ways, for example:

- Ecosystem disruption
- Species extinctions
- Agricultural impacts
- Populations displacement
- Premature deaths
- Disease incidence
- Disruption of water supplies

One word that is commonly used to describe this crisis is "existential," referring to a change that could threaten the basic welfare of the earth. Polls indicate that there is a strengthening public attitude for the need to move away from fossil fuels and toward a low carbon world economy. Reducing greenhouse gas emissions implies high costs today and high benefits, in the form of reduced climate change damages in the future. Estimating any of these types of damage means working through a sequence of risks and probabilities, of climate events, and social and economic factors. From an economic standpoint, one way of measuring future impacts of climate change is in terms of lost economic productivity. This is especially relevant in developing countries, where economic security is still elusive for millions of people. With predicted changes in the global climate, how much will world Gross Domestic Product (GDP) be reduced, as compared to what it would have been without these changes?

Estimates of future damage depend on assumptions about how much change there will be in the future global temperatures. A recent review of economic studies concludes that with a rise in mean temperature of 3°C, global GDP would drop by about 1.6 percent by the end of the twenty-first century, while if the mean temperature increases by 6°C, income would be reduced by about 6.5 percent. These are income changes, so they do not include effects that do not register on income. Non-market impacts of climate change are of concern, especially those of biodiversity loss and population displacements. In addition, these are averages, and there is high concern about the possibility of low probability but extreme events.

A useful way of talking about future damages is with what is known as the social cost of carbon (SCC). The SCC is the estimated future damages per marginal tonne of CO_2 emitted today. This may be a useful number, even considering the extreme difficulties of estimating future damages. As a single number it can be used to evaluate the benefits and costs of contemporary programs that affect the quantity of emissions. The larger the future damages, the higher is the SCC, and vice versa. Current estimates of the global cost of carbon are $50 to $60 per tonne of CO_2, depending on the discount rate used.

Damages and discounting

Reducing global emissions of greenhouse gases has high costs in the near term and benefits that accrue well off in the future. When evaluating these possible programs in a benefit-cost framework, discounting plays an important role. Discounting, as we discussed in Chapter 5, is a way of comparing monetary amounts that occur in two different time periods. Among economists there is controversy about comparing the up-front costs of reducing CO_2 emissions today with the future benefits in terms of reduced climate-caused damages. Some argue that the discount rate should be near zero; while others argue that future values should be discounted by a higher rate like something approaching the average return to productive investments. These two approaches lead to different conclusions about the ultimate shape of the damage function from global climate change. A low discount rate yields a future damage function shaped something like Case A in Figure 10.1.

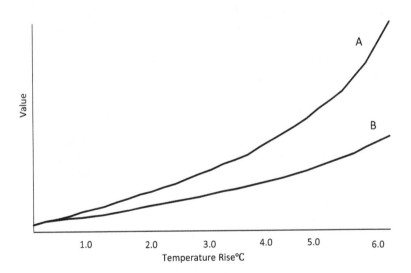

Figure 10.1 Alternative damage functions

A higher discount rate, of say, five percent, yields a damage function looking like Case B in the figure. Case A has the feature that at some higher concentration level damages increase very rapidly. A shape like Case B might follow from studies of the impacts of "routine" climate change. By routine we mean a substantial but gradual climate change that human societies can adjust to within the capacities of modern economies. It does not rule out huge, even catastrophic, changes for some who live in vulnerable parts of the world, such as low-lying coastal plains. Questions naturally arise about the possibility that at some point during a gradual change the world could experience an abrupt and unforeseen change. A further question, about which virtually nothing is known to date, is whether the optimal response to expected routine climate change in any way affects the probabilities of abrupt climate events.

The response profile

Since there is uncertainty about the damage function for atmospheric GHG, there is uncertainty about what level of emissions the world should strive for. The long-run objective is to moderate the increase in the concentration of greenhouse gases in the earth's atmosphere, and then to decrease the concentration to a "safe" level. In the Paris Agreement it was agreed that steps should be taken to hold the increase in mean global surface temperature to no more than 2°C. This was a target for rallying countries around a specific objective. Behind it is the authority of the United Nations Intergovernmental Panel on Climate Change (IPCC). To reach the target it will be necessary to stop the growth in global GHG emissions, then bend the growth curve downward.

An alternative approach to setting a fixed 2°C target is to examine different emission control plans in a benefit-cost framework. The costs are the abatement costs of switching energy systems away from fossil fuels, as well as reducing the other types of greenhouse gases. The benefits are the reduced future damages stemming from temperature changes. Different emission reduction plans would produce different global temperature profiles. This approach would give us a way of addressing a key question: what is humanity's optimal response profile to the global climate change problem? Should we take immediate and maximally aggressive steps to reduce carbon emissions and harden our economies to the threat? Or should we take more modest actions today, perhaps working to shift out of fossil fuels over the next decade, and plan on adapting to the climate changes that do happen? Or should our action plan be something between these two courses of action? These trade-offs are fundamental to how we identify an optimal plan. The question is not whether we should move to reduce GHG emissions, but how fast we should move to limit GHG emissions.

The alternative damage functions shown in Figure 10.1 correspond to two emission control plans, which are shown in Figure 10.2. The damage function that rises more steeply corresponds to a more stringent emission reduction plan, such as Plan A in Figure 10.2. The flatter damage function of Figure 10.1 corresponds to a less stringent emission control profile, that of Plan B in Figure 10.2.

Plan A shows a program in which there is concentrated effort in the short run to slow the increase in GHG concentration and global temperature. A maximum concentration is reached fairly early on, then gradually diminishes as the various greenhouse gases dissipate in the long run. Plan B shows a reduced short-run effort to control emissions, with the maximum atmospheric concentration and temperature reached later and a bit higher than with Plan A. Plan A represents an aggressive program in the short run. Plan B shows a more gradual approach with lower costs in the short run and benefits accruing more in the future. It might seem easy to choose the program with earlier impacts, but this is a more costly course of action. And the question is whether some of the early costs of Plan A should better be devoted to investments that increase economic welfare and security for people who then would be better able to cope with climate changes in the future.

Both of these time plans are "optimal," in the sense that they are regarded as efficient over the next 200 years or so. They both get to zero GHG

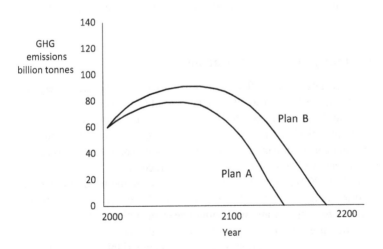

Figure 10.2 Alternative emission reduction scenarios

emissions, and a low GHG concentration, but they do it in different time scales. One (A) says concentrate heavily on reducing GHG emissions in the shortest time possible. The other (B) says don't concentrate exclusively on short-run emission reductions; invest also in productive capital, including capital for adaptation purposes, that will enhance the economic welfare of disadvantaged populations. The choice between these two options needs to be made by policy makers, not by economists.

If we did a benefit-cost analysis of emission reduction according to these two plans, the result would be strongly affected by what we used for a discount rate. If we use a low rate to evaluate future benefits of emission reduction we would lean toward plan A, as is the case with many who believe this is the preferable course of action. If we use a standard somewhat higher discount rate, we would lean toward plan B, which is the preferred course for many others in this debate.

A justification for a rapid response comes from the simple notion that these are future damages from inaction, but that some of these damages could be catastrophic. A reason for adopting a more deliberate course of action today is that it would take advantage of present efforts to spur the development of technology to move economies away from fossil fuels.

One factor that has not been given sufficient attention is the impact of climate change on natural capital. Natural capital is the totality of naturally occurring features of the world, including geology, soil, water, air, and all living organisms. The human values of some of these are registered in their role as consumptive and non-consumptive inputs in the economy. An important consideration is how changes in natural capital will impact the welfare of an increasingly urbanized human population and the ecosystems themselves.

The need for global collective action

Countries are not equally affected by changes in the climate, or equally responsible. Table 10.1 shows 2019 data on total CO_2 emissions, per capita emissions, and emissions per dollar of GDP, for the top ten countries in terms of total emissions. The importance of these numbers is to show that, if there is to be a significant attack on this problem, some type of collective action is necessary. Of course, this is widely recognized, but with limited results to date (2021). Action has been hampered by the need to transform the historic energy systems of the world, and by differences of opinion about who is responsible and who should bear the major costs.

International efforts to address climate change started with the United Nations Framework Convention on Climate Change (UNFCCC), agreed to in 1992. The agreement elevated the importance of the problem and set in

Table 10.1 Emissions of CO_2 of top ten countries, 2019

Country	Total CO_2 emissions (Mtonnes)	% of global CO_2 emissions	CO_2 emissions per capita (tonne CO_2/cap)	CO_2 emissions per GDP (tonnes CO_2/1,000$)
China	11,535	30.0	8.1	0.51
United States	5,107	13.4	15.5	0.25
European Union (28 – with UK)	3,304	8.7	6.5	0.14
India	2,597	6.9	1.9	0.28
Russia	1,792	4.7	12.5	0.45
Japan	1,154	3.0	9.1	0.22
Germany	703	1.9	8.5	0.16
International Shipping	730	1.9	–	–
South Korea	652	1.7	12.7	0.30
Saudi Arabia	615	1.6	18.0	0.38
Global	38,017	100	4.9	0.29

Source: European Commission, https://edgar.jrc.ec.europa.eu/overview.php?v=booklet2020.

motion efforts to negotiate an active international response. The UNFCCC recognized "common but differential responsibilities and respective capabilities in light of different national circumstances." Pursuant to this convention, the Kyoto Protocol was negotiated. It came into force in 1997, covered six greenhouse gases, most notably CO_2, and established target emission levels that countries were obligated to reach during the period 2008–2012. The targets were in terms of aggregate (i.e., national) anthropogenic carbon dioxide equivalent (CO_2e) emissions, expressed as a percentage of 1990 country emissions. Twenty-one countries met their emissions targets. However, these were not major emitting countries, so global emissions continued to increase in the absence of any concerted effort by major emitting countries to enforce their national targets. A major stumbling block was the disagreements between developed and developing countries.

The next effort was the Paris Agreement, negotiated in 2015. The intention was to get away from the centralized approach of Kyoto to a decentralized system in which initiative shifts to the individual countries. According to Paris, each country is to put forth its own "Nationally Determined Contribution" (NDC) for reducing greenhouse gases, outlining the specific steps it would take to do so. The stated advantage of the approach is that it allows each country to rely on its own circumstances, capabilities, and priorities to craft an individual response. The NDCs are required to be updated every five years.

The GHG content in the world's atmosphere is a public good, as are most environmental features. It is available to all countries on equal terms and cannot be reduced by one country's action without being reduced for all countries. The upshot of this is that, in trying to mount collective action to reduce GHGs, there is a tendency and a temptation for individual countries to "free ride" on the efforts of others. Free riding is an attempt by a participant to garner the benefits of an agreement (or a good or activity) without paying their rightful share of its costs. In the case of a global climate agreement, free riding implies attaining the benefits of GHG cutbacks by other countries without bearing the costs of reducing emissions in one's own country. No country will announce itself outright as a free rider. Instead, the tendency will be to support an agreement but fail to take any concrete implementation steps. If enforcement is not feasible through existing international institutions, might there be new structures that could accomplish it? Perhaps an agreement where certain trade benefits are withheld from countries that engage in free riding.

Equity issues

Having almost 200 nations meet to negotiate a global plan of action immediately raises equity issues. What is a fair distribution of the burden of moving to a non-carbon-based energy system? These are fairness questions and matters of environmental justice that have to be addressed within the policy processes of each country. One principle, that mirrors the intracountry situations, is that economically less developed countries should not be disproportionately burdened by a global GHG emission reduction. A burden that a developed country can easily meet may be much more costly, in proportion, in a developing country. Such would be the case, for example, if identical emission reduction targets were set in every country. Developed countries should, therefore, pay a larger share of the costs of GHG reductions. This could be done in several ways. They could be asked to reduce their emissions proportionately more than developing countries (which would affect the overall global cost of reductions); or developed countries could compensate developing countries for emission reductions. Another approach is to follow the precedent set in the Montreal Protocol, giving developing countries longer time periods to make adjustments in their GHG emissions.

Another relevant rule is the "polluter pays principle": that the costs of pollution control should rightfully be placed on the people who are responsible for it. By that measure, it is the developed world that has had the main benefit of inexpensive fossil fuels to power their development paths. This is another reason for concluding that the developed world should be the one that absorbs the largest part of the global costs of GHG control. It is clearly the case where consideration of efficiency and cost-effectiveness should give way to the need for an equitable global response.

National mitigation responses

The Paris Agreement essentially shifts the initiative to the countries of the world, to act individually or in groups. Countries must devise targets and action plans and have some means of monitoring and reporting results. To reduce the use of fossil fuels there has been a natural tendency to fall back on technology standards and command-and-control policies. Many countries, for example, have established fuel economy standards for cars and trucks, with the goal to reduce the consumption of fuel derived from fossil sources. Some states in the US have instituted renewable fuel mandates for electricity generating plants. Some EU countries have established renewable energy targets.

There is widespread recognition that the first step in shifting the energy sector is ending the subsidies for fossil fuels. Around the world a huge variety of fossil fuel subsidies have been put in place over the years, covering every phase of the industry: exploration, development, extraction, refining, bulk transportation, and consumption. Many reasons have been given for subsidizing the industry: supporting a critical industry, benefiting consumers, energy independence, spurring economic development, reducing the risk faced by fossil fuel producers, and others.

We have discussed subsidies and their effects earlier (Chapter 8). Subsidies on energy markets have the effects of increasing the income of fossil fuel operations and of lowering prices paid by consumers. They therefore increase the demand for fossil fuels, which obviously works exactly opposite to the objective of lowering GHG emissions. On the other hand, subsidies for the adoption of renewable energy technologies are widely favored because of their putative effect in reducing GHG emissions. Studies have shown, however, that subsidies for specific technologies (e.g., biofuels) produce dubious benefits when the account is taken for all the market and regulatory interactions that result. This is especially true when subsidies are activated through provisions of public tax codes. Tax advantages for fossil fuel operators are ubiquitous. For example, in the US firms may write-off exploration costs, and in many countries they may reduce taxes through a depletion allowance, on the theory that extraction reduces the value of quantities left in the ground.

Some of the national plans adopted under the Paris Agreement have focused on taking steps to decrease energy intensity or decrease carbon intensity. Implications of these can be seen in the expression shown in Figure 10.3.

Energy intensity is essentially the amount of energy used per unit of GDP. When it refers to the energy consumption of a particular item, such as a light bulb or a washing machine, it is sometimes called energy efficiency.

Energy Intensity

$$Total\ carbon\ emissions = N \quad x \quad \frac{GDP}{N} \quad x \quad \frac{C}{GDP} \quad x \quad \frac{E}{C} \quad x \quad \frac{CO_2}{E}$$

Carbon Intensity

Figure 10.3 Energy/carbon intensity. Where: N is the number of people in a country. GDP is the gross domestic product (total output) of an economy. C is the total consumption expenditures in the country. E is the total energy consumption. CO_2 is the greenhouse gas emissions

Carbon intensity is essentially CO_2/C, the amount of CO_2 produced per unit of consumption expenditure (C) (found by multiplying the last two terms together). We note that carbon intensity can be decreased without decreasing carbon emissions, by holding these emissions constant and increasing aggregate consumption expenditures. This, of course, would have zero impact on global climate change. Another factor of interest is the last one, CO_2/E, which shows how much carbon is being produced per unit of energy consumed. A cutback in the ratio shows a degree of decarbonization, but it leaves out the importance of reducing energy consumption itself. Dividing both sides of the equation by N, total population, yields the average carbon footprint for the individuals in this population.

A common country goal has been to declare a future date by which the country would become "carbon neutral." Carbon neutral goals are also made by communities, schools, private firms, and organizations. Carbon neutrality is determined by the balance of carbon emissions and carbon sinks, that is, when

carbon emissions – carbon sinks = 0

carbon neutrality is attained. The move toward neutrality can be done by either reducing carbon emissions or by increasing carbon sinks. A natural carbon sink is an environmental feature that absorbs and captures atmospheric carbon, so that carbon does not disperse into the atmosphere and add to global warming. The biggest carbon sinks are growing vegetation, especially trees, soil, and oceans. Artificial carbon sinks are human-devised technologies that can extract carbon from the atmosphere and hold it in isolation. Artificial sinks are landfills and carbon-capture and storage procedures.

Carbon neutrality plays into the concept and market for carbon offsets because carbon neutrality of a single source can be reached not by decreasing carbon emissions, but by increasing one's holdings of carbon offsets. There has been a vigorous growth in international carbon offset markets. This includes markets for compliance offsets and markets for voluntary offsets. An institutional structure for offsets has developed, which includes firms and agencies whose job is to develop and maintain the necessary market functions for transferring offsets, as well as organizations that supposedly vouch for the authenticity of offsets. Offset prices are widely variable, depending on location of the offset producing project, whether or not they are based on forestation projects, and other factors.

International offsets were officially endorsed in the Clean Development Mechanism of the Kyoto Protocol. In this system, some countries could get credit for moving toward their own emission reduction requirement by financing emission reductions in other countries. This feature is also included in the Paris Agreement. Offsets can be incorporated into cap-and-trade programs; the European Trading Scheme, for example, allows some trades to be consummated by the purchase of carbon offsets.

As mentioned above there is wide consensus that steps should be taken to reduce GHG emissions and drive the atmosphere levels of these gases to much lower levels. A controversial aspect of this is the cost. From a regulatory standpoint there is a general consensus among environmental economists that incentive-based policies can substantially lower the overall cost of addressing climate change. Or, to say the same thing in a different way, for a given amount of spending we could get a substantially greater effect by using incentive-based policies. As we have discussed, there are two candidates for this: cap-and-trade and a tax on carbon. Both of these plans have the effect of putting a price on carbon. With emissions charges the effect is direct. With a cap-and-trade plan it is indirect; here restricting the quantity of emissions works through abatement costs to put a price on carbon. The effect of putting a price on carbon is to raise the price of goods and services according to the carbon footprint of each. This is illustrated in Figure 10.4. A carbon price, established "up-stream" where fuels are first supplied, will filter through the market system, most heavily affecting goods with a large carbon footprint and least heavily, goods or services with a small carbon footprint.

The importance of this is that it sends a price signal through the economy, leading people (consumers, businesses, venture capitalists, inventors, nonprofit organizations, etc.) routinely to make decisions based in part on their implications for carbon emissions.

Emissions trading

As we discussed in Chapter 9, emissions trading is a way of cost-effectively lowering total emissions. Cap-and-trade works by creating permits, or

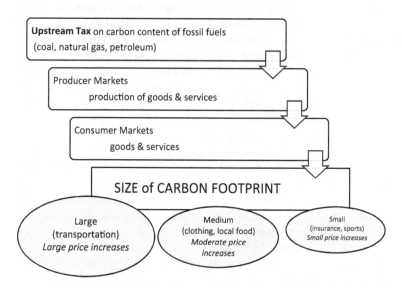

Figure 10.4 A tax on carbon

allowances, equal in number to the desired level of total emissions, distributing these to participating sources, and then allowing permit trading that will lead to a cost-effective redistribution of emissions among sources. The market price for permits that are established in trading becomes, in effect, the price for the emission of a tonne of carbon. Cap-and-trade by now has a substantial policy history. The most extensive CAP program for reducing CO_2 emissions is the European Trading Scheme (ETS). Emission trading systems have been started in Australia, New Zealand, China, and Korea.

Enough experience has been had with carbon trading systems to provide lessons and guidelines for future design and utilization. Important lessons are the following:

1. The original allowance of tradable permits must usually be done without detailed knowledge of abatement costs. This means that it is easy to award too many permits, as happened in the ETS, or too few. The result is either a permit price that is too low, or too high, relative to some unknown number that represents the efficient price.
2. There are equity and political issues in how allowances are distributed. If they are given out free, there is the sense that valuable property rights to pollute are being awarded to polluters themselves. In many plans, permits are auctioned by public agencies, leading to public revenue.

3. The essence of efficient and cost-effective control of carbon emissions is that emitting sources all end up at the same marginal abatement cost. For this to happen there must be an opportunity of free and unlimited trading of permits among sources. In particular, there must be the opportunity to trade among sources and across time. These features are called banking, where permits for one time period can be saved for use and used in a future trading period.

Carbon taxes

The other way of pricing carbon emissions is with a carbon tax. When fuels are burned the amount of CO_2 going into the air is strictly proportional to the carbon content of the fuel. Thus it is feasible to place a tax on fuels according to their carbon content. As of 2020, carbon taxes have been put in place by 64 countries and 35 sub-national jurisdictions, covering about 22 percent of global GHG emissions.

As an incentive-based policy, a carbon tax recommends itself because it puts a price directly on emissions. Conversely, cap-and-trade sets quantities, which emission trading then converts into a price on carbon. This has led frequently to low and volatile prices for permits, while carbon pricing gives less price volatility risk. Setting taxes is often a politically fraught process, and carbon taxes will invariably be involved in that conflict. Some of the countries that have set carbon taxes are shown in Table 10.2.

For social efficiency, carbon taxes should be set equal to the marginal costs of carbon emissions. While carbon is a global externality, the damages from climate change will vary from one country to another. If carbon prices in each country are set according to damages in that country, we might expect diversity in tax rates as indicated. The great variation in actual carbon prices around the world seems to indicate that other considerations loom large in setting the tax rate. In particular, carbon

Table 10.2 Carbon taxes (US$/tonne CO_2e)

Country	Carbon tax (US $/tonne CO_2e)
South Africa	7.00
Canada	35.00
Chile	5.00
Denmark	26.00
Iceland	30.00
Portugal	23.60
Sweden	119.00

Source: World Bank Group (2020), *State and Trends of Carbon Pricing*, Washington, DC.

taxes yield a source of public revenue, so it is reasonable to suppose that the policy controversies about carbon taxes centers to some extent on their revenue aspects, such as how a government spends the carbon tax revenue, rather than their carbon-reducing aspects.

A factor that looms larger in carbon taxes is their potential impact on consumers, especially consumers with low or moderate incomes. As with all price increases, the price increases that follow a carbon tax are regressive. It needs to be remembered, however, that the damages resulting from a changing climate are also likely to be regressive. Suggestions have been made by economists and others to accompany carbon taxes with reductions in taxes elsewhere, so the regressive effects of the carbon taxes are offset. Another option may be to recycle the revenues from carbon taxes into direct income support for certain consumers.

Another factor that has worked against the acceptance of carbon taxes is the effect of price increases on the competitive position of the affected firms. The effect will be to weaken the competition positions of these firms. A way around this in international trade is for countries to put a tax on the carbon content of imported goods. The difficulty of this is for the importing country to be able to determine what that content actually is.

Leakage may also be a problem, though perhaps not more than it would be with any other type of public carbon-reducing policies. Leakage refers to the idea of production shifts, away from places where carbon taxes are put in place, toward locations where they are not. This will be regarded as a loss of economic productivity in the region losing production; it will also be a loss for the whole effort to reduce global carbon emissions.

We have mentioned earlier (see Chapter 4) that environmental regulation ought to be judged in part on its ability to provide the incentive for creating and adopting new pollution-control technologies. The essence of putting a price on carbon is to create that incentive. A carbon tax gives firms a strong incentive to develop more carbon-efficient technologies as a way of lowering costs. The revenues from a carbon tax can also be devoted to subsidizing research in low-carbon production technologies, and in atmospheric carbon-removal technologies.

The ultimate social cost of addressing this problem will depend on whether action incorporates fundamental ideas of cost-effectiveness. This means, for example, giving precedence to techniques that have relatively lower abatement costs. Relying on a carbon price, perhaps one that rises slowly over time, has a better chance of achieving this than relying on a succession of emission standards and technology specifications that arise out of the pushing and shoving of an ongoing political struggle.

It is now clear that an effective attack on the global greenhouse effect, via the decarbonization of the world's economies, has three main dimensions:

1. Major initiatives in developing new technologies, those for producing power without the need for fossil fuels, and those for extracting atmospheric carbon from past emissions.
2. Providing each individual citizen with an incentive that will encourage them to lead their everyday lives with a lower carbon footprint. This means increasing the price of carbon, as discussed previously.
3. Finding some means by which the less economically developed countries of the world can be part of the decarbonization effort while responding to their citizen's desires for economic growth.

The economics of adaptation

It appears that mitigation strategies, especially GHG emission reductions, will not be soon enough or strong enough to ward off significant change in the global climate. Unless there is a major technological discovery of a way to reduce atmospheric carbon, a major burden will fall on human adaptation.

Adaptation will consist of some combination of individual and collective action. Individuals will take actions based on their understanding of the risks of certain conditions and the costs of protecting themselves against those risks. Accurately assessing risks has never been a particularly strong human trait, and the risks of climate-induced events will confront people with new possibilities. A central role of public agencies will be to convey risk information accurately to help moderate the natural tendency among people to discount future risks too heavily, thereby prioritizing the more immediate. We have stressed in this book the importance of incentives, the configuration of personal benefits and costs that lead people toward, or away from, efficient and equitable social decisions. Critical to this is the extent to which individuals are asked to bear the risks of climate change: more and more severe storms, higher temperatures, greater fire probabilities, etc.; or whether those risks are shifted to society in general. Who will bear the higher risks of living in flood-prone areas, for example?

Public participation in global climate change will be prominent through investments in infrastructure. The question is whether these will be undertaken in an atmosphere of emergency response, or whether they will be the result of prior planning and with suitable emphasis on cost-effectiveness. Among some communities there is a growing stress on resiliency planning. Resilience is the idea of maintaining a functioning community in the face of climate challenges, and for expedient community recovery from a disaster. This will include physical infrastructure, and regulation changes (e.g., land-use regulations) that climate challenges will make necessary.

There is another possible strategy for dealing with global climate change, especially the possibility that we might encounter some extreme values for climate and the damages caused by its alterations. This is to take actions today that will forestall what we expect to be the most likely future climate impacts. But if we should encounter unexpected extreme values, in temperatures and other factors, we are likely to resort to geoengineering to deal with them. Geoengineering means taking deliberate steps to alter the energy balance of the earth, or a large portion of it, so as to promote cooling. For example, introducing materials into the atmosphere that would block a certain amount of the incoming radiation. The expected costs of these types of action are likely to be small, at least relative to the costs of global GHG emission reduction. The impacts may be large, but uncertainty about them, especially the possibility of inadvertent or uncontained impacts, make geoengineering speculative at this point in time.

Further reading

Barrett, S. (2007), "The Incredible Economics of Geoengineering," *Environmental and Resources Economics*, Volume 39, pp. 45–54.

Goulder, L.H. and A. Schein (2013), *Carbon Taxes vs. Cap and Trade: A Critical Review*, National Bureau of Economic Research, Working Paper 19338, Cambridge, MA.

Metcalf, G.E. (2019), "On the Economics of a Carbon Tax for the United States," *Brookings Papers on Economic Activity*, Spring 2019, pp. 405–458.

Nordhaus, W.D. (2013), *The Climate Casino: Risk, Uncertainty, and the Economics of a Warming World*, Yale University Press, New Haven, CT.

Stern, Nicholas (2006), *The Economics of Climate Change – The Stern Review*, The University of Cambridge Press, Cambridge, UK.

Tirole, J. (2017), *Economics of the Common Good*, Princeton University Press, Princeton, NJ and Oxford.

Wagner, G. and M.L. Weitzman (2015), *Climate shock: The Economic Consequences of a Hotter Planet*, Princeton University Press, Princeton, NJ.

Index